THE SWEDISH INVESTMENT RESERVE

A DEVICE FOR ECONOMIC STABILIZATION?

By Martin Schnitzer

July, 1967

PUBLISHED AND DISTRIBUTED BY THE

AMERICAN ENTERPRISE INSTITUTE
FOR PUBLIC POLICY RESEARCH
WASHINGTON, D. C. 20036

———————◆———————

Martin Schnitzer is Professor of Business at Virginia Polytechnic Institute and is editor of the Virginia Social Science Journal. He has published two studies on public policy in Europe for the Joint Economic Committee of the U.S. Congress, and has also published a study on Soviet economists for the U.S. Office of Education. He is the author of several journal articles and business cases, and is currently working on a comparative economic systems text. He has been the recipient of a number of grants, including three to do research in Europe.

———————◆———————

Price: $2.00

AMERICAN ENTERPRISE INSTITUTE
For Public Policy Research

THE AMERICAN ENTERPRISE INSTITUTE FOR PUBLIC POLICY RE-
SEARCH, established in 1943, is a nonpartisan research and educa-
tional organization which studies national policy problems.

Institute publications take two major forms:

1. LEGISLATIVE AND SPECIAL ANALYSES—factual analyses of current legislative proposals and other public policy issues before
   the Congress prepared with the help of recognized experts in
   the academic world and in the fields of law and government.
   A typical analysis features: (1) pertinent background, (2) a
   digest of significant elements, and (3) a discussion, pro and
   con, of the issues. The reports reflect no policy position in
   favor of or against specific proposals.

2. LONG-RANGE STUDIES—basic studies of major national problems of significance for public policy. The Institute, with the
   counsel of its Advisory Board, utilizes the services of competent
   scholars, but the opinions expressed are those of the authors
   and represent no policy position on the part of the Institute.

PREFACE

It is the purpose of this study to examine the effectiveness of the Swedish investment reserve fund as an instrument for economic stabilization. The subject is timely for the reason that there has been increasing public acceptance in the United States of the theory that government fiscal measures—changes in spending and taxes—are useful tools to help regulate fluctuations in the level of economic activity. This theory, which can be called "push button" fiscal policy, is the cornerstone of the "new economics" as followed and practiced by the Council of Economic Advisers in the Kennedy-Johnson Administrations.

The idea in back of "push button" fiscal policy is that the level of aggregate demand can be changed via changes in spending or taxes. If the economy needs stimulating, taxes can be cut or suspended, assuring an increase in total demand and hence an increase in the level of economic activity; if the economy needs depressing, the same taxes can be raised or restored, causing a decrease in total demand and the level of economic activity. A prime example of "push button" fiscal policy is the suspension and restoration of the investment tax credit.

The effectiveness of "push button" fiscal policy is contingent upon the prompt response of the economy to changes in spending or taxes, and also upon promptness in the timing of the fiscal action. There is little to indicate that prompt response and timing are present in the American economy. The recent restoration of the investment credit is a case in point. Restored by the House, the investment tax credit languished in the Senate for several weeks.

I would like to express appreciation to the American Philosophical Society for supporting research in Sweden which served as background for this study.

A recent symposium held by the American Enterprise Institute debated the merits of "push button" fiscal policy. Critics of the "new economics" contended that erratic and inappropriate fiscal and monetary policies have been responsible in part for economic instability in the United States. Evidence was also submitted that fiscal policy actions have been poorly timed in recent years.

The Swedish investment reserve is a fiscal device which is designed to stimulate investment during a recession and discourage it during a boom period. However, its use is normally associated with the former, and it will be examined primarily within that context.

The use of the investment reserves brings to mind the quotation in the Book of Genesis: "Behold there come seven years of plenty throughout all the land of Egypt. And there shall arise after them seven years of famine." In the familiar biblical story, Joseph's solution to the feast and famine problem was to construct huge storehouses into which grain and foodstuffs collected during the seven good years were deposited. During the seven years of famine, the stores of grain and foodstuffs provided the reservoir that was necessary to sustain the populace.

In essence, the investment reserve attempts to do the same thing. In periods of prosperity, business firms are encouraged through the medium of tax incentives to set aside a certain amount of their liquid funds in a reserve which will not be used until needed. In a period when there is a downturn in economic activity and unemployment occurs, the resources are then released for the purpose of stimulating investment and employment.

The investment reserve has been used as a countercyclical instrument on three occasions. In 1958 and 1959, the reserve was released to encourage investment during the recession. In 1960 and 1961, the total amount of the investment reserve was neutralized as an anti-inflationary measure, and in 1962 and 1963, the reserves were released for the second time to counteract a recession. The reserve is normally identified as an anti-recessionary measure.

On several occasions in the 1950s, Sweden used a direct tax on investment as an anti-inflationary device. The investment tax, or duty, was a flat tax of 10 or 12 percent on most investment made during a given year. It was a temporary tax, levied in certain years and then withdrawn when the Swedish government felt that investment was consonant with the level of economic activity. The tax was discontinued in 1958 and has not been used since.

Both devices—the investment reserve and the investment tax—represent an attempt to influence the level of aggregate demand by manipulating one of its components, namely investment. Sweden has also used very liberal rules for inventory valuation and liberal depreciation schedules on machinery and equipment to strengthen the financial position of business firms during periods of economic decline.

Sweden has been a forerunner in the development and use of fiscal devices aimed at attaining full employment and economic growth. These devices show a rather sophisticated degree of resourcefulness on the part of the Swedish government. However, in view of the interest in the use and timing of anticyclical devices in this country, it is interesting and enlightening to find out just exactly how well these devices work when put to the acid test. This is what this study purports to do.

CONTENTS

COUNTERCYCLICAL TAX POLICY

Introduction

Increasing concern over inflationary dangers inherent in the economic situation of 1966-67 has prompted considerable interest in the subject of countercyclical tax policy. Hearings held before the Subcommittee on Fiscal Policy of the Joint Economic Committee stressed the need for and design of temporary tax changes which can be put into effect immediately in response to a need for preventing inflation or appreciable unemployment.[1] Three major topics were discussed: contributions of rapid tax changes to stabilization, criteria for such tax changes, and technical design.

The conclusions of the participants can be summarized as follows: fiscal policy is important as a device for economic stabilization. Changes in taxation and government spending can influence output, prices, and employment. As countercyclical measures, the automatic stabilizers—the personal income tax, corporate income tax, unemployment compensation, et al.—have proved successful.[2] Direct changes via legislative enactment—the investment credit of 1962 and the tax cut of 1964—have also demonstrated the effectiveness of fiscal action.

However, there has been criticism of existing procedures for changing federal taxes on the ground that the time consumed by the process seriously reduced the possible usefulness of tax changes as a stabilization tool. The time factor is a major defect in fiscal policy. A considerable hiatus exists between the points in time when the need to take action is recognized and actual execution of fiscal action is taken.

---

[1] See "Tax Changes for Short Run Stabilization," Hearings before the Subcommittee on Fiscal Policy of the Joint Economic Committee of the U. S. Congress, 89th Congress, 2d Session, 1966.

[2] Wilfred Lewis, *Federal Fiscal Policy in the Postwar Recession* (Washington: The Brookings Institution, 1962).

1

Inflation or unemployment may well have been exacerbated by the time that action is taken.

The Joint Economic Committee has considered measures to permit greater flexibility in fiscal policy.[3] These measures involve prompt variations in tax rates. Of the measures considered, the Joint Economic Committee favored a uniform percentage addition to or subtraction from corporate and personal income tax liabilities computed under permanent provision of the tax code. This tax change would be temporary and would be tied to a standard format which could be based on formula flexibility, presidential discretion, standby legislation, or an abridgement of current procedure.

Suggestions for new types of taxes or variations of existing ones were advanced by participants at the hearings, with the idea that improvements could be made in short-run stabilization policy. Among these suggestions were: the use of a spending-savings tax which would be applied to consumption when restraint in the economy is needed and to saving when stimulation is needed; a tax on inventories which would discourage accumulation by business firms; and raising or lowering the cost of holding working capital through variations in interest payments allowed as a deduction against business income.

The temporary suspension of the 7 percent investment credit in 1966 was designed to have a direct effect on investment.[4] The original intent of the credit was to encourage net additions to the stock of machinery and equipment. It permitted firms to deduct each year from their tax liability 7 percent of their investment outlays on equipment subject to limits. In effect, the government paid a subsidy on investments by giving back to firms a fraction of their investment cost through this special tax credit.

However, in March, 1967, the investment credit was restored by the House of Representatives. The reason for the restoration is the anticipated decline in the rate of investment in new plants and equipment during 1967. A reduced rate of investment was indicated in the House Ways and Means Committee report which said that plans for new plants and equipment for 1967 indicated an increase of 3.9

[3] See "Tax Changes for Short Run Stabilization," A Report of the Subcommittee on Fiscal Policy of the Joint Economic Committee of the U. S. Congress, 89th Congress, 2d Session, 1966.

[4] Administration bill (HR 17607) provided a 16-month suspension of the 7 percent tax credit on business investment and of authority for accelerated tax write-offs on depreciation of industrial and commercial buildings. The provisions of the bill formed a part of a broader program designed to curb inflationary pressures in the economy. The other features of the program included a reduction in the growth of government expenditures.

percent above the 1966 level, as opposed to a 16.7 percent increase between 1965 and 1966.

As a countercyclical fiscal instrument, the investment credit is subject to serious criticism. There is one conflict between the long-term goal of the investment credit, which is to promote modernization and growth, and the short-term goal of checking inflation. Moreover, it is impossible to quickly turn on and off the stream of capital expenditures, since investment decisions can only be translated into positive final action over long periods. It also can be argued that removal of the credit is more likely to accelerate price inflation than to dampen it, because expansion of production capacity is slowed when increasing demand is pushing prices upward. Suspension of the investment credit also means that the cost of capital goods will rise from 93 percent to 100 percent of the purchase price—a cost increase of 7.5 percent.

The investment credit has been criticized on the grounds that it represents a deliberate attempt to depart from tax neutrality. The tax system is being deliberately used to get businessmen to change their decisions to undertake more investment than their judgment would otherwise dictate.

When the investment credit was proposed, critics contended that once in effect it would inevitably be manipulated for economic control purposes. This contention was denied by spokesmen for the Kennedy Administration, who insisted that the credit was designed to be a permanent feature of the tax system, and that its purpose was to raise the average level of investment. There was no intent to employ it as a countercyclical device.[5]

---

[5] Although the restoration of the investment credit passed in the House of Representatives by a 386-2 roll call vote, this does not constitute an affirmation of faith in the efficacy of the investment credit as a countercyclical fiscal instrument.

Congressman Wilbur Mills, chairman of the House Ways and Means Committee, indicated that quick changes in business investment incentives will not become a habit as far as he is concerned. He states as follows: "We must not let ourselves be placed in the position of raising or lowering the hemline of taxation, from season to season, merely to make the merchandise more saleable. It is essential that our tax laws have a certain degree of stability, if our system of voluntary tax collection is to continue to function effectively."

John W. Byrnes, ranking Republican on the committee, accused the Johnson Administration of having a "yo-yo tax policy," and charged that the committee had been used in an inappropriate effort to manipulate the economy.

In view of the moderate growth in output in the third quarter of 1966, it is quite probable that the decision to suspend the investment credit could have been postponed until January, 1967. At this time, it was more apparent that a decline in investment activity would occur in the latter part of 1967, and the administration would have saved itself the trouble of suspending and restoring the investment credit. It is likely that the decision to suspend the credit was

4

Tax measures which are designed to suppress or encourage investment may reduce or increase consumption through the multiplier
effect. Also, measures designed to discourage or encourage consumption spending will have a direct effect on investment through the
accelerator effect.[6] To choose between measures designed to affect
consumption and measures designed to affect investment, however,
is difficult. From the standpoint of timing, certainty, and reversibility,
the personal income tax is probably the best countercyclical tax
measure to use. The personal income tax is not a major factor in
corporate business planning; it is broadly based; and the rate can be
easily varied and changes can take effect promptly through with-
holding.

However, the effectiveness of any stabilization policy—fiscal or
monetary—depends to a major degree on timing. All too often,
stabilization measures, if taken at all, are taken only after the need
for them has become apparent.[7]

Fiscal policy changes involve five time lags.[8] The first lag involves
the time lost between the recognition of the need for action and the
initiating of it; the second lag is in the process of legislative action;
the third lag involves changes in the flow of expenditures; the fourth
lag involves the change in consumer and investment demand for
output brought about by the fiscal changes; and the fifth lag involves
the change in output which is brought about in response to a change in
consumer and investment demand. A time period of a year or more
can elapse before the fiscal change actually makes its effect on the

based on political as opposed to economic considerations. After all, a tax
increase before election time, even though it may be warranted as an anti-
inflationary measure, is hardly likely to be embraced by politicians and the
public with any enthusiasm.

[6] Attempts to quantify multiplier and accelerator effects of tax changes are
fraught with dangers. However, the Joint Economic Committee in the 1963
Annual Report, pp. 45-55, estimated the multiplier-accelerator effects resulting
from a $10 billion tax cut.

[7] One has only to look at current stabilization policy in the United States.
The rather belated effort to suspend the investment credit, and hesitation to
raise taxes, until after the election in the fall of 1966, reflects not only inappropriate timing, but the basic weakness of fiscal policy—the unwillingness of
politicians to raise taxes or cut government spending—even though these measures may be absolutely necessary. Fiscal policy, to be effective, must work two
ways: as a stabilizing device during both periods of unemployment and declin-
ing output, and during periods of full employment and rising prices. Reductions
in taxes, increases in government expenditures, or both, can compensate for a
lack of total aggregate demand during unemployment; increases in taxes,
reductions in government spending, or both, can offset too much demand during
an inflationary period.

[8] Commission on Money and Credit, Stabilization Policies, Research Study
One, *Lags in Fiscal and Monetary Policy* (Englewood Cliffs, N. J.: Prentice-
Hall, 1963), pp. 3-11.

economy. A basic desideratum of fiscal policy is to find the appropriate devices that can reduce the time lags in operation.

In a parliamentary system, such as Sweden's, fiscal policy measures can be effected within a shorter period than is possible in America. In Sweden, for example, the Ministry of Finance can carry out appropriate fiscal policy measures independent of control by the Swedish parliament. The budget, once disclosed by the Ministry of Finance, is almost certain to be accepted by parliament.

In the American legislative system, fiscal policy changes usually face a time-consuming process. Bills introduced by individual members of the Congress are likely to be pending for many months and no one can be sure of the extent to which they will be amended. Administrative proposals also must face the legislative machinery. Hearings are usually held and changes in the proposals are made to make them acceptable to Congress and to interested pressure groups.

As an anti-inflationary measure, tax devices to restrict investment have proved to be more popular in many western countries than tax devices to restrict consumption. The reason, at least in the United States, is pragmatic: it is politically more desirable to penalize investment than consumption.

Government Measures to Influence Investment

The Canadian government, concerned with inflationary pressures in the economy, adopted two temporary measures designed to restrain investment.[9] Four factors were instrumental in selecting these measures:

1. The promptness with which each could be brought into effect;
2. The provision of prompt pressures upon and inducements for business to defer capital expenditures;
3. No addition to production costs is brought about with the adoption of the measures; and
4. The measures should help business firms to maintain capital expenditures in future years. Each measure can be terminated on short notice without serious effects, should the economic circumstances change rapidly.

The first measure was put into effect by the government in an amendment to the Income Tax Regulations. It reduced the deprecia-

---

[9] See House of Commons Debates, Volume 111, Number 51, 1st Session, 27th Parliament, Ottawa, March, 1966, pp. 3375, 3387, and 3395.

tion allowances that can be claimed for various classes of capital assets acquired during the period April, 1966, to October, 1967—about 18 months. The measure applies to most kinds of buildings, machinery, and equipment, but not to heavy construction equipment, pipelines, or the generating and distributing equipment of public utilities.

The other temporary measure is designed to divert and immobilize a modest portion of the flow of funds that is the major source of finance for the capital expenditures of businesses. It is a refundable tax on cash profits, payable by most corporations, and by certain types of trusts on specified types of income. The basis of the tax is taxable income of the company for the current year, less the income tax payable thereon, plus depreciation allowances deducted in determining income. In determining the tax base, deductions of debt payments which have an original term of three years or longer under written loan contract are permitted. The tax is 5 percent of adjusted net income less debt payments.

The refundable tax is payable monthly for a period of 18 months. The amount received under this measure will be repaid, with interest at 5 percent, after an interval of 18 to 36 months after receipt.

Some countries have experimented with variations in depreciation allowances as a countercyclical measure. To stimulate investment during a recession, depreciation allowances are increased; to retard investment during boom periods, depreciation allowances are lowered. The United Kingdom changed its depreciation allowances upward and downward during the 1950s in an attempt to fit investment spending to current business conditions. There is evidence that this policy was effective to some degree, chiefly through the incentive aspects of depreciation.[10]

Similar actions were taken in Canada and West Germany during the same period. In the Canadian case, however, the postponement of depreciation was for nonessential projects only.

There seems little doubt that countercyclical variations in depreciation allowances would have some impact on investment, because one result is to raise a business firm's tax bill in the immediate period (inflation is presumed) and lower it in the next period when profits are lower. Some economists have advocated reliance on changes in

---

[10] Richard Bird, "Countercyclical Variations of Depreciation Allowances in the United Kingdom," *National Tax Journal,* March, 1963, pp. 41-53.

depreciation allowances as a permanent instrument of tax stabilization policy.[11] However, its use presents several problems, notably from the standpoint of timing and equity. The time lag between the decision to increase or decrease the depreciation allowance and the decision by business firms to postpone or increase investment may be considerable. Also there would be discrimination in favor of business firms that acquired assets in a period immediately before a decrease in depreciation allowances is put into effect, and against firms whose assets are wearing out and have to be replaced during the period in which decreased depreciation allowances are in effect. The same reasoning applies to the suspension of the 7 percent investment credit.

Therefore, to be most effective as a countercyclical measure, and consistent with other goals, increases or decreases in depreciation allowances, or suspension of the investment credit, should apply to all investment spending that occurs after the change is made, and also to investment spending on projects started before the change is made.[12]

Sweden has been a pioneer in the field of countercyclical tax policy.[13] An important measure—the investment reserve—has been used in an attempt to maintain an adequate level of investment throughout the country. The measure is rather unique and has been used to counteract both unemployment and inflation. It was used in the recessions of 1958 and 1962, and in the inflation of 1960 and 1961.

A direct tax on investment has also been used as an anti-inflationary device. It was used several times in the decade of the 1950s when inflationary pressures were prevalent in the Swedish economy. However, it was replaced by the investment reserve for reasons that will be explained later.

---

[11] Alvin Hansen advocates countercyclical depreciation policies. See *Economic Issues of the 1960's* (New York: McGraw-Hill, 1960), pp. 51-52.

[12] For a recent review of some of the issues involved in variations in depreciation allowances, see Delmas D. Ray, "Some Economic Aspects of Depreciation Accounting," *The Quarterly Review of Economics and Business,* February, 1962, pp. 59-69. Also see the House Ways and Means Committee publication, "Tax Revision Compendium," 1959, pp. 793-99.

[13] The World Tax Series volume, "Taxation in Sweden," makes this statement: "No country has sought more vigorously to use taxation, together with other fiscal, monetary, and regulatory measures, as a tool to affect the business cycle. Sweden has employed pioneering income tax devices designed at least in part to make the economy more resistant to depression and to influence the propensity of business to invest; in this way it has sought to enlist private capital in the task of leveling the business cycle." P. 69.

8

Economic Policy in Sweden

As was stated in the preface, this study seeks to examine the effectiveness of the investment reserve and the investment tax as countercyclical tax instruments. Particular emphasis will be placed on the investment reserve which has been used in recent years. However, it is first necessary to discuss the economic policy objectives of the Swedish government in order to provide a suitable framework for the analysis of the investment reserve.[14]

The central objective of economic policy in Sweden is the maintenance of full employment. This objective stems from circumstances which prevailed in Sweden between the two World Wars. The average unemployment rate in the period 1923-30 was 11 percent; in the period 1930-33, the unemployment rate was 19 percent; and in the period 1933-37 the average rate was 16 percent.[15] In the period 1929-39 the average unemployment rate was 16 percent.[16]

However, Sweden has had a very high level of employment in

---

[14] Contrary to what many Americans think, private enterprise is dominant in Sweden. Ninety-one percent of all industrial enterprises are privately owned. Private enterprise accounts for 87 percent of the gross national product and employs 89 percent of the labor force. The Swedish government has constantly stimulated private investment through a liberal depreciation system.

Government ownership is largely limited to railroads, telephone, telegraph, and other utilities. There is one government-owned steel mill, located in northern Sweden, which was built to stimulate local employment. However, private enterprise accounts for 93 percent of steel production. The automobile and shipbuilding industries are privately owned. Private enterprise also accounts for 92 percent of chemical production, 86 percent of food production, and 95 percent of forest production. The banking system is, with a minor exception, privately owned.

See "Unemployment Programs in Sweden," by Martin Schnitzer, Joint Economic Committee, Congress of the United States.

[15] Erik Lundberg, *Business Cycles and Economic Policy* (Cambridge: Harvard University Press, 1957), p. 52.

[16] The unemployment rate in Great Britain during the same time period affords an interesting comparison. In 1921 it was 17.8 percent; in 1922 it was 16.2 percent; and in 1923 it was 12.2 percent. In 1930 the unemployment rate was 19.9 percent. Broken down into the various regions, the unemployment rate was as follows: London—9.8 percent; The Midlands—18.6 percent; Northeast—24.5 percent; Northwest—29.3 percent; Scotland—23.5 percent; and Wales—31.2 percent. In 1932 the national unemployment rate was 21.9 percent, and in the period 1933-37 the average unemployment rate was 14.2 percent.

Post-World War II economic policy in Great Britain and Sweden stems from the economic conditions that prevailed in each country between the wars. An emphasis on maintaining a high level of employment regardless of the economic consequences characterizes both countries. There is also a strong emphasis on social welfare; each country has a myriad of social welfare programs which are designed to protect the people from the vicissitudes of life. One may wonder, however, whether the pendulum has swung too far in this direction. Apparently it has in Great Britain as evidenced by the current austerity measures of the Wilson government.

general since the Second World War. Unemployment has averaged less than 2 percent since the war, and the supply of labor in some areas is so short that many workers have been brought in from other countries.

It is necessary to point out, however, that Sweden has been rather fortunate in that nonparticipation in the Second World War insulated her from the problems of reconversion and redevelopment which confronted most other European countries.

The general economic policy of the Swedish government has been to achieve a high level of employment. Monetary and fiscal policies have been subordinated to this objective. Throughout most of the postwar period, the Swedish economy has labored under inflationary pressures as the government has pursued a cheap money policy as an integral part of its full employment and social welfare program. When a general decline in economic activity occurs, a series of employment measures are used, including emergency public works, extra government orders from industry, and accelerated building construction.[17]

Nevertheless, certain problems exist in the Swedish economy. Seasonal unemployment, ranging several points above the average annual unemployment rate has prevailed since the end of the war. Long-term structural changes have been taking place in several industries—textiles, forestry, clothing, and shoes and leather—and have caused pockets of unemployment. The upgrading of skills requirements in response to improved technology has resulted in the unemployment of many semiskilled and unskilled workers. Finally, the export-oriented nature of the economy makes Sweden vulnerable to a decline in exports.

Unemployment has been a problem in northern Sweden, particularly among the forest workers. In January of 1962, the unemployment rate in Sweden was 2.1 percent; however, in the two northernmost provinces—Norbottenslän and Vasterbottenslän—the unemployment rate was 6 and 6.3 percent respectively. In February of 1965, the unemployment rate for the two provinces was 5.9 percent compared to the national average of 1.7 percent.[18]

As might be expected, seasonal unemployment exists to a major degree in Sweden, particularly in the construction industry. Unem-

---

[17] Schnitzer, *op. cit.*, pp. 43-49.

[18] Unemployment is measured on a monthly basis. The percentage unemployed is based on the registered number of unemployed within the unemployment insurance system.

ployment rates during the months of December, January, and February run two to three times above the annual average.

Although overall unemployment has been kept at a level of less than 2 percent over the last decade, the full and overfull employment in much of the country has put pressure on the price level. The problem, at least over the last five years, has been to control inflation. The consumer price index has shown an average increase of approximately 5 percent a year since 1960. The average wage rate increase over the same period of time has been 6 percent a year. In terms of real wages, the average Swedish worker has achieved only a small increase since 1960.

The table below presents changes in the consumer and wholesale price indices since 1958. A marked increase in each price index has taken place in the last two years. The Swedish government has instituted restrictive monetary policies, which, at least as of the present, are having little effect on the inflationary pressures which are prevalent in the economy.

TABLE I. WHOLESALE AND CONSUMER PRICE INDICES FOR SWEDEN

1949 = 100%

Year	Wholesale Price Index	Consumer Price Index
1958	144	152
1959	144	153
1960	148	159
1961	151	163
1962	154	170
1963	159	175
1964	166	181
1965	173	190
1966 (August)	178	201

Sources: Konjunktur Laget, Reviderad National Budget, 1966, pp. 149-50; Quarterly Report of the Skandinaviska Banken, September, 1966, p. 1.

Conclusion

Tax devices to stimulate investment have been used as an instrument of economic policy in a number of countries. All sorts of liberalized depreciation schemes, investment allowances, and tax exemptions have been tried. The basic reason for the use of these devices is to stimulate growth through the stimulation of investment.

Investment change, however, can be a major cause of economic instability. Too much investment at a level of full employment can contribute to inflation; too little investment during a downturn in economic activity can contribute to unemployment.

Some countries have experimented with discretionary tax policies which are aimed at smoothing out or regulating the volume of investment to a point that is consistent with prevailing economic conditions. A prime example of such policies is the Swedish investment reserve which has been used as a countercyclical instrument on several occasions.

THE INVESTMENT RESERVE

Introduction

The investment reserve is a device, incorporated in the Swedish tax structure, designed to help iron out economic fluctuations by encouraging private corporate savings in periods of high profits and private capital expenditures in periods of unemployment. Companies are encouraged to set aside part of their pretax profits in a reserve, and if these funds are disbursed for investments in buildings, machinery, and inventories during a period when investment is desirable for employment purposes, substantial tax privileges are obtainable.

The investment reserve law was enacted in 1938. The basic intent of the legislation creating the reserve was the provision of a tax device which, by permitting postponement of taxation, would enable companies to build up reserves for use in the event of a future depression as a source of investment and hence employment. However, it has been put to practical use as an instrument of fiscal policy only in the past eight years.

The investment reserve possesses flexibility in that it can be used without the approval of parliament. This reduces considerably the lapse of time that accompanies legislative enactment of fiscal policy measures. Decisions to utilize the reserve are made jointly by the Labor Market Board and the Ministry of Finance. Implementation of the investment reserve is the responsibility of the Labor Market Board.

The Labor Market Board is responsible for the implementation of employment policy in Sweden. It is a tripartite group consisting of representatives from labor, management, and the Swedish government. There are two representatives from the Swedish Employer's Confederation, two representatives from the Swedish Trade Union

Confederation, one representative from the Central Organization of Salaried Workers, one representative from the Confederation of Professional Associations, one representative for female workers, one representative for agriculture, and three representatives from the government.

The Board has the responsibility for putting into operation various employment-creating measures, such as supervision of the investment reserve funds. It is also responsible for the operation of the public employment service, planning of projects suitable to be carried out as emergency public works, direction of the start and discontinuance of such works, licensing of starting permits for buildings, and stimulating occupational and geographical mobility of workers.

The Labor Market Board is also responsible for economic forecasting. Forecasts are based on county labor board surveys of business and employment conditions which are made twice a year. These surveys include data on the amount of incoming orders, volume of production, inventories, planned investment in buildings and machinery, unfilled vacancies, and expected layoffs or increases in personnel.

Investment Reserves

Companies are permitted to set aside, at their own discretion, up to 40 percent of pretax income as an investment reserve for economic stabilization.[1] This amount is deductible from income for the purpose of both the national and local income taxes.[2] Forty-six percent of the amount must be deposited in a non-interest-bearing account in the Central Bank of Sweden (Riksbank), and the remaining 54 percent remains a part of a company's working capital. No government permission is needed to set aside this reserve. However, control over the use of the reserve is exercised by the Labor Market Board.

For example, assume a pretax income of 2,500,000 kronor

---

[1] Actually, there are two types of investment reserves—investment reserves for forestry and investment reserves for business. The paper is concerned with the latter only.

[2] Swedish corporations are subject to both national and local taxes on income. The national income tax is levied on corporations at a flat rate of 40 percent. The local income tax, averaging 15 percent, is levied at a flat rate on all corporations. The amount of the local income tax assessed during the year against a corporation is a deduction which is subtracted from net income to give the assessable income for national income tax purposes. The effective tax rate—national and local—is approximately 49 percent:

$$\frac{15.100}{100} + \frac{40.85}{100} = 49 \text{ percent}$$

($480,000). A company may set aside one million kronor as an investment reserve. Forty-six percent of this amount (460,000 kronor) must be set aside in the Riksbank and is, in effect, neutralized until needed during a downturn in economic activity. The remaining 54 percent (540,000 kronor) belongs to the company as a part of ordinary working capital. The company may use this amount for any purpose at any time it so desires.

Uses of Investment Reserve Funds

The purposes for which an investment reserve can be used are as follows:

1. To write off the cost of erecting, enlarging, or reconstructing a building; however, the amount that can be written off in a tax return must not exceed the expenditure actually in the fiscal year, a condition which applies also to the other types of investment.

2. To contribute toward the erection, enlargement, or reconstruction of dwellings of present or former employees of the corporation.

3. To defray the cost of repair and maintenance of buildings which are used in their regular activities by corporations engaged in mining or manufacturing.

4. To write off the cost of machinery and other equipment intended for permanent use which have been purchased or of vessels which have been purchased or rebuilt during the fiscal year.

5. To cover the cost of the repair of vessels.

6. To depreciate stocks of raw materials and of semifinished and finished products up to an amount equal to the expenditures for the production or procurement of stocks during the fiscal year.

7. To cover the costs of prospecting and other preproduction work during the year in mines, quarries, and similar deposits under exploitation.

8. To promote the sale abroad of commodities which the corporation produces in Sweden. This use of investment reserves, however, is subject to special authorization.[3]

---

[3] The investment reserve regulations for industry were amended on July 1, 1963, to make provisions for an inventory investment account. Under this provision, firms may be allowed to transfer in their investment accounts, their investment reserve or a part of it, to an "inventory investment account," for a period of four years. During this period, a firm may be allowed to dispose of the corresponding amount of the reserve deposited in the Riksbank, thereby improving its liquidity position. The firm is entitled to a special investment deduction of 10 percent, computed on the amount by which the value of all inventories has increased during the period in question. The deduction, how-

The 46 percent of the reserve in the Riksbank and the remaining 54 percent, which is a part of working capital, may be released for any of the above purposes when the Ministry of Finance considers economic conditions to be worsening.[4] The reserves are to be released during a recession when they are needed to stimulate investment. The significance of the reserves lies in the fact that up to 100 percent of an investment can be written off immediately. When the investment reserve is used for the permissible purposes, the amount used is not restored to taxable income, but the asset charged to the reserve is not subject to depreciation allowance.

Several examples of how the investment reserves may be utilized are as follows:

1. Assume, as in the previous example, that a company has set aside one million kronor as an investment reserve.[5] Forty-six percent has been deposited in the Riksbank in a special non-interest-bearing account. The remaining 54 percent has been charged to working capital. The company has used the 54 percent in the operation of the business.[6]

A downturn in business activity occurs. The Ministry of Finance decides that the time is propitious for the release of the investment reserves.[7] It notifies the Labor Market Board to this effect. The

---

ever, cannot exceed 10 percent of the amount transferred to the inventory investment account. After the prescribed period, the transferred amount must be brought back to taxation, but a firm can neutralize this by making new allocations to investment reserves.

[4] A corporation establishes an investment reserve by debiting its profit and loss account and crediting the Investment Reserve account.

[5] The Swedish currency unit is the krona. One krona is worth $.19. One million kronor would be approximately $190,000. To convert kronor into dollars, divide the amount of kronor by five to obtain a close approximation of the dollar amount.

[6] It is left to the company to manage its liquidity position with a view to the needs of a possible release. Thus, when reserves are released, the company must have on hand—or be able to raise—more than half of the amount it is required to invest.

[7] The decision, in essence, is a joint one. The Ministry of Finance, on the basis of forecasts and consultation with the Labor Market Board, makes the decision to release the investment funds. The Labor Market Board is responsible for the implementation of the release of the funds. It notifies firms with investment reserve funds that the funds can be utilized for investment. When the permission to use the funds has been granted by the Labor Market Board, the blocked funds are released to the firms by the Riksbank (Bank of Sweden).

The time lag between recognition of the problem and implementation of stabilization policy, although reduced by the elimination of the cumbersome legislative process, still is subject to human errors in forecasting and decision making. However, the recognition lag itself is reduced considerably by a system for advanced information on impending employment changes which is based on agreements between the Labor Market Board and different employer associations.

Labor Market then gives permission to individual companies to use their investment reserves for any of the purposes previously mentioned.[8]

The company decides to use the entire one million kronor for the purchase of new equipment. It may withdraw the entire 460,000 kronor which it has on deposit with the Riksbank. As for the remaining 540,000 kronor which has been kept in the business and used, the company must reproduce this amount, because it is a part of the investment reserve.

2. Assume, however, that the company decides to use only a part of the total reserve; for example, 100,000 kronor. The company has to take 46 percent of this amount (46,000 kronor) from its deposit in the Riksbank. The amount of its deposit is reduced by 46,000 kronor, and the remainder is 414,000 kronor (460,000-46,000). As for the remaining 54 percent of the amount (54,000 kronor), the company must produce this amount. It is deducted from that part of the investment reserve (540,000 kronor) which has been retained by the company and which has been charged to working capital. When this deduction has been made, the original amount has been reduced to 486,000 kronor (540,000-54,000).

Not only is the investment reserve not restorable to taxable income, but in order to stimulate the use of this program even more, an extra investment deduction—10 percent of the reserve used—is permitted in the tax assessment in its next income tax return.[9]

For example, assume that a company sets aside one million kronor in an investment reserve fund in 1960. In 1962 a recession occurred, the reserve funds were released, and the company used its entire amount for new equipment. Ten percent of this amount (100,000 kronor) was deductible from pretax income in 1963. Assume a pretax income of three million kronor. The 100,000 is deductible from this amount, and the income for tax purposes is now 2,900,000 kronor.

If an investment reserve is used without the authorization of the Labor Market Board, the amount involved plus a penalty of 10 per-

[8] Permission can be given in several ways. One alternative is to grant general permission to all firms that have set up investment reserves. Permission, however, can be restricted to certain industries or local areas, where the rate of employment is expected to be low. Another alternative is to grant permits by approving individual applications, specifying the projects for which the applicants wish to use the investment reserve. This method was used during the recessions of 1958-59 and 1962-63.

[9] In other words, a company which uses its investment reserves in 1962 is permitted to deduct 10 percent of the amount from taxable profits in its income returns for 1963.

cent of the reserve is added to taxable income during the next assessment period.

For example, assume the company in the aforementioned example decides to use its entire investment reserve (one million kronor) without the authorization of the Labor Market Board. This amount plus a penalty of 10 percent (100,000 kronor) is restored to taxable income.[10]

There is general permission after five years have elapsed, irrespective of business conditions, to withdraw up to 30 percent of the reserves provided they are used for the allowable purposes. However, in this case a company will not receive the extra 10 percent investment deduction.

For example, assume a company set aside one million kronor as an investment reserve in 1958. In 1963—a good year for the Swedish economy—the company decides to utilize part of its reserve to purchase machinery. It may use up to 30 percent of its reserve (300,000 kronor) for the acquisition. It decides to use this amount. Thirty percent of the amount on deposit in the Riksbank (460,000 kronor) can be withdrawn. This amounts to 138,000 kronor. Thirty percent of the reserve kept by the company (540,000 kronor) may also be withdrawn. This amounts to 162,000 kronor.

Through the system of investment reserves, the government has been able to influence a countercyclical movement of private investment. An increase in the investment reserve serves the purpose of dampening boom conditions for the reason that investment spending will be postponed.[11] This postponement of investment spending reduces the level of aggregate demand. The release of the investment reserve during a recession has the effect of stimulating investment. Companies utilize their investment reserves, on various investment projects, thus raising the level of aggregate demand.

The 46 percent sterilization reserve in the Riksbank has an important advantage from the standpoint of business cycle policy in that the reserve cannot be invested before permission to do so has been obtained from the Labor Market Board. This, however, assumes that the Labor Market Board possesses an unusual degree of omniscience from the standpoint of the appropriate timing of the release of the funds.

---

[10] Needless to say, this does not happen frequently.

[11] There will be a loss of tax revenue to the government. If this results in deficit financing by the government to finance the various social welfare programs, the effect would be to circumvent the intent of the investment reserve.

During the boom of 1960 a further inducement was added to the investment reserve program. If a firm wished, it could pay into the Riksbank an amount equal to 100 percent of the reserve. A tax rebate was granted, which was as follows:

1. If a company placed its reserve with the Riksbank before August 1, 1960, it could deduct from its taxable income during this year an amount equal to 12 percent of its reserve.

2. If the reserve was placed in the Riksbank between August 1 and November 1, 1960, the corresponding deduction was 8 percent.

The amount of the reserve in excess of the required 46 percent was repayable at the end of 1961. However, in 1961 boom conditions again prevailed and companies which had deposited the full amount of their reserves to the Riksbank in 1960 were granted a further inducement to leave them in for another year or until the end of 1962.[12] The deduction permitted from taxable income in 1961 was 10.5 percent of the full reserve.

Tax deductions similar to those of 1960 were given to companies in 1961 if they agreed to deposit the full 100 percent of the reserve in the Riksbank. A tax deduction of 12 percent was given if a deposit was made before July 1, 1961, and 8 percent if a deposit was made before October 1, 1961, with 54 percent of the deposit repayable at the end of 1962. This tax deduction could still be claimed if the reserves were released for authorized purposes.

Tax Advantages of the Investment Reserve

Although the tax advantages to be derived from the use of an investment reserve are illustrated in more detail in the appendix, they can be briefly summarized:

1. An advantage is gained when a company sets aside the 46 percent for deposit in the Riksbank. In the original example, the company set aside in the total investment reserve fund an amount of one million kronor out of a pretax income of 2,500,000 kronor. Forty-six percent was deposited in the Riksbank, and the remaining 54 percent was kept by the company. The company initially retains the difference between the income tax (49 percent of the income) and the amount deposited in the Riksbank (46 percent of the investment reserve), or, in the example, 490,000 kronor (49 percent

---

[12] In fact, a recession did occur and the reserves were released.

of one million kronor) less 460,000 kronor (46 percent of one million kronor). The difference of 30,000 kronor represents an initial gain to the company.

2. When the reserve is used (assume the full amount of one million kronor), the company is entitled to an extra investment deduction of 100,000 kronor from taxable income in the next tax year. Since the tax rate is 49 percent, the company saves 49,000 kronor.

3. In certain cases, the investment may be written off at once by the amount withdrawn from the reserve.[13]

However, these advantages to the corporation must be compared to the gains which would have accrued from the normal liberal depreciation allowances which could have been used.[14] The net advantage is the difference between the advantages obtained with an investment reserve and those obtainable through the use of normal depreciation allowances.

Allocations to Investment Reserves

Although investment reserve provisions have been in effect since 1938, the original law was regarded as experimental in nature and funds allocated to reserve accounts were negligible in magnitude. However, important changes in the law were made in 1947. Companies were allowed to set aside up to 20 percent of net income as a reserve for future investment, deductible from income for both the national and local income tax. All a company had to do was to allocate the reserve to its accounts; no physical segregation in an account in the Bank of Sweden was required.

However, there was criticism of the 1947 legislation for the reason that the tax-free retention of the reserve increased corporate liquidity during periods when the economy was operating at full capacity. Temporary legislation during the early 1950s suspended the right

---

[13] It should also be mentioned that for major projects requiring up to two years for completion, the government can authorize not only the use of existing reserves, but also future allocations to the investment reserve. In either case, a ceiling of 75 percent of the project is set. The total amount a company can be authorized to draw on existing reserves and future allocations must not exceed 75 percent of the total cost of the project. This means that a company can write off up to 75 percent of the cost of the project as soon as the expenditure is made, instead of the far smaller depreciation allowances permitted. However, government authorization is required. The project must be justified from the standpoint of public policy, unemployment, and the public welfare.

[14] See the Appendix which is at the end of the study for comparison of advantages.

to make allocations to investment reserves, except in special situations.

In 1955, new legislation again permitted the use of deductible investment reserves. The amount of net income that could be allocated to an investment reserve was increased to 40 percent. However, 40 percent of the amount allocated had to be deposited in a special non-interest-bearing blocked account in the Riksbank. The remaining 60 percent could be retained by the company. In 1957, the amount that had to be deposited in the blocked account was changed to 46 percent to bring it in line with the effective national and local income tax rates.

Prior to 1947, allocations to investment reserves were negligible. The liberalized provisions of the 1947 legislation caused an increase in allocations to the investment reserves, and by the end of 1955, Swedish corporations had set aside approximately 247 million kronor in reserves under the provisions of the 1947 law. However, a marked increase in allocations to investment reserves occurred during the 1955-61 period. Although a large percentage of the reserve had to be deposited in the Riksbank, increased tax benefits well compensated companies for this inconvenience.

Allocations to investment reserves for the period, 1955-63, increased considerably over the pre-1955 period. The largest allocation occurred in 1960, when the entire amount (100 percent reserve) had to be deposited to blocked accounts in the Riksbank. The annual average in recent years has been around 500 million kronor.

The data presented below show recent allocations to the investment reserve.

Year	Allocations (Millions of Kronor)
1955	167
1956	125
1957	215
1958	419
1959	530
1960	1,063
1961	520
1962	439
1963	521

The Investment Reserve in Denmark and Finland

Although the investment reserve is a uniquely Swedish institution, modified variations exist in Denmark and Finland. Since 1957 Danish corporations and individual proprietorships have been permitted to create investment reserves through special tax-free deposits of up to 15 percent of profits, representing advanced depreciation of certain capital goods. When these goods are acquired later, a write-off equal to the amount deposited is made, leaving the balance subject to general depreciation procedures. It is a condition for such deposits that 50 percent of the amount must be paid into a blocked account at the Central Bank of Denmark. All deposits must be used within ten years. Any portion of the deposits, which has not been used within the ten-year period is subject to a penalty equal to 5 percent of the deposited amount per annum.

However, the investment reserve fund has been used more as a device to stimulate economic growth and also industrial development in northern Denmark than as a countercyclical tax instrument.

In Finland, no more than 50 percent of the annual pretax income shown on the accounts of corporations may be transferred into an investment reserve fund. The investment fund is deposited in a blocked account in the Bank of Finland. Unlike the Bank of Sweden, the Bank of Finland pays interest on all investment funds deposited in blocked accounts. Permission to use the funds is given by the Ministry of Finance for the following purposes:

1. For the construction or basic improvement of factories or storage facilities, or for social and housing facilities for employees;

2. To purchase machines or equipment, including ships and railway equipment, made in Finland;

3. For the cost of working a mine, quarry, peat bog, or any other comparable property;

4. For drainage or cultivation of forests and the construction of forest roads;

5. For the cost of vocational training of manpower;

6. For the cost of distribution of Finnish products in foreign countries; and

7. For any purpose which is approved by the Ministry of Finance and which promotes employment.

Interest on the blocked account is based on the lowest discount rate of the Bank of Finland, and for federal tax purposes is not considered as taxable income. Moreover, the investment fund, when utilized for any of the above purposes, is not subject to the national income tax. For the year in which the investment fund is used, the corporate taxpayer is also entitled to an extra deduction from taxable income of an amount of 12 percent of the investment funds that were used. For example, assume that a Finnish corporation spent 100,000 finnmark of investment funds in 1965; 12,000 finnmark would be deductible from pretax income.[15]

Summary

The primary objective of investment reserve policy is to stimulate private industry's propensity to invest during a recession. Although the policy attempts to curb investment activity by reducing the liquidity of business firms during a period of high economic activity, the allocations to investment reserves, in themselves, do not reduce a firm's ability to invest over time, in cash flow terms, since an amount approximately equivalent to what otherwise would have been paid in income taxes is sterilized in the Bank of Sweden. The allocations to the reserve have a neutral effect on investment.

When the investment reserve was introduced in 1938, the intention of the law was to create funds which would be set aside as a reserve to combat future depressions. The postponement of taxation would enable business firms to build up reserves which could be used in the event of a depression as a source of funds for investment and hence of employment. At the time the investment reserve provisions were introduced, Sweden was recovering from the depression of the 1930s, and use was being made of other tax devices, including free depreciation, for the purpose of stimulating private investment.

However, the first use of the investment reserve as a counter-cyclical instrument occurred as late as 1958. There are two reasons for this time lapse: 1) the original law did not make it financially worthwhile for firms to delay investment; and 2) World War II and postwar European recovery intervened to make the Swedish economy enjoy almost 20 years of unprecedented prosperity. In 1955 the law was revised to provide new incentives to set aside investment reserves, and require firms to deposit a portion of the reserves in a blocked, non-interest-bearing account at the Riksbank.

---

[15] The finnmark is exchanged for the U. S. dollar at a rate of 3.21 finnmark to $1.

The investment reserves were released in 1958-59 and in 1962-63. One-hundred percent sterilization of the reserves was accomplished in 1960 and 1961. The overall effects on employment and investment will be analyzed in the following chapter.

APPLICATION OF THE INVESTMENT RESERVE

Introduction

The first time the investment reserve was released for the purpose of economic stabilization was during the 1958-59 recession. In 1960-61, the entire reserve (100 percent) was sterilized in the Riksbank as an anti-inflationary measure and during the 1962-63 recession, the investment reserve was released for the second time.

The Release of the Reserve in 1958-59

The investment reserve was released to stimulate investment during the recession of 1958-59. Permission to use the reserves was granted in May, 1958, and was terminated in September, 1959.

The 1958 recession in the United States and the major European countries adversely affected employment in Sweden's export-oriented industries. The deterioration in the export markets for the products of the forest industry was the major cause of unemployment. The recession also affected the textile and shoe industries.

The following table indicates the variations in monthly unemployment rates in Sweden during 1957-59.[1] These fluctuations reflect seasonal variations in unemployment which are considerable.

---

[1] For the measurement of unemployment in Sweden see "Measuring Employment and Unemployment," President's Committee To Appraise Employment and Unemployment Statistics, pp. 250-51.

Unemployment in Sweden is measured by taking those unemployed who are members of unemployment insurance societies and expressing their number as a percentage of the total number of members in the societies. Since the members of these societies make up only 36 percent of the total labor force, reliance is also placed on periodic sample surveys.

TABLE II. UNEMPLOYMENT RATES, BY MONTHS, FOR SWEDEN, 1957-59

(In percent)

Year	Jan.	Feb.	Mar.	Apr.	May	June	July	Aug.	Sept.	Oct.	Nov.	Dec.
1957	2.9	2.6	2.6	2.7	1.9	1.2	.8	.9	.9	1.2	1.7	2.7
1958	3.8	3.6	3.6	3.8	2.6	1.3	1.0	1.3	1.3	1.7	2.4	3.3
1959	4.3	3.4	2.6	2.7	1.9	1.2	1.0	1.2	1.2	1.3	1.6	1.8

Source: Sammanställning Arbetsmarknadstabeller, Kungl Arbetsmarknadsstyrelsen, Stockholm, October, 1963.

The percentage unemployed is based on the number of registered unemployed within the unemployment insurance system. Sample surveys of the labor force are also taken to gain more complete information about the number of the unemployed. The estimate of the total percentage of all unemployed as opposed to the actual percentage of insured registrants who are unemployed indicates an upward revision is necessary in the percentages in the table. For example, the estimated unemployment rate for all workers in November, 1961, was 1.7 percent compared to 1.2 percent for workers covered by unemployment insurance. To adjust Swedish unemployment rates to American definitions, an upward adjustment of about 0.3 to 0.5 percent is necessary.

General permission was given for the release of forestry reserves. The Labor Market Board prescribed the condition that forestry projects financed through the use of the reserve had to be finished before June 30, 1960.

However, more circumscribed permission was given for the release of the investment reserves for business. A basic criterion for permission to use the reserves was that projects should be started at times which corresponded with the highest rate of unemployment. This criterion was particularly applicable to investments in buildings, with the basic objective to start the construction during the winter months when unemployment was the highest. Projects also had to conform to a time schedule approved by the county labor boards. The money involved could be utilized only during a certain period. The length of the period depended on the size and nature of the project.[2]

Altogether 418 companies received 613 permits from the Labor Market Board to dispose of 695,300,000 kronor ($133,000,000) during the period from May, 1958, to September, 1959. Additional permits for 320,000,000 kronor ($61,000,000) were given for long-term projects, because in certain cases companies were allowed to use current reserves and future allocations to reserves.

---

[2] The obvious concern was with the timing and duration of projects. There was the danger that the duration of many projects would be longer than the duration of the recession. Therefore, the length of most projects was fixed at 1 and 1½ years.

The following table presents a breakdown of the use of investment reserve funds, by industries, during the period from May, 1958, to September, 1959. The largest proportion of the fund used involved investments in buildings and plants.[3]

TABLE III. DISTRIBUTION OF RESERVE FUNDS, BY INDUSTRY, MAY, 1958 TO SEPTEMBER, 1959

Industry	Number of Enterprises	Percent	Estimated Use of Funds (Million Kronor)	Percent
Bruksforetag[1]	8	1.9	86,1	12.4
Mines	4	1.0	3,8	.5
Metal and Machinery	136	32.5	279,7	40.2
Earth and Stone	17	4.1	5,5	.8
Wood Products	29	6.9	36,2	5.2
Pulp and Paper	32	7.7	90,2	13.0
Graphic Trades	9	2.1	7,5	1.1
Food Processing and Beverages	22	5.3	18,2	2.6
Textiles	41	9.8	27,2	3.9
Leather, Hair, and Rubber	8	1.9	10,3	1.5
Heavy Chemical	27	6.5	27,5	4.0
Power Stations	4	1.0	10,7	1.5
TOTAL (Mining and Manufacturing)	337	80.7	602,9	86.7
Commerce	53	12.4	70,4	10.2
Transportation	18	4.3	18,1	2.6
Other	11	2.6	3,6	.5
TOTAL	418	100.0	695,3	100.0

[1] Bruksforetag, a very old form of enterprise, combines agriculture and forestry with one or several kinds of industrial enterprise; e.g., mining.

Source: Gideon Nitare, "Investment Reserves," Division for Industrial Locations and Investigations, National Labor Market Board, January, 1961, p. 10.

Employment Effect

The employment effect of the release of the investment reserve was felt primarily in the construction industry. This industry is affected to a major degree by adverse climatic factors in the winter months, which cause seasonal unemployment, particularly in Stockholm and the larger cities. Investment funds which were released to cover the

---

[3] Approximately 90 percent.

cost of constructing buildings usually carried the stipulation that work done on buildings should be started at such a time that would as sufficiently as possible contribute to the maintenance of employment during the winter months.

Employment derived from the use of the investment reserve funds during the 1958-59 period was as follows:[4]

1. In November, 1958, 2,000 workers were employed on building projects financed with investment reserve funds. Total unemployment in Sweden during that month was approximately 100,000. The 2,000 workers represented about 8 percent of the total number of workers employed in building construction.

2. In February, 1959, the number of workers employed on building projects financed with investment reserve funds had increased to 4,000. This amounted to 17 percent of the total number of workers employed in building construction.

3. In August, 1959, the number had increased to 6,400. The maximum employment-creating effect from the use of the investment reserves was derived during this period which lasted through the fall and winter of 1959-60. However, this maximum effect was not achieved until a considerable time period had elapsed after the original permission had been given to use the investment reserves.[5]

4. In February, 1960, 6,300 workers were employed on projects financed with investment reserves [6]—21 percent of the total employed in building construction.

Timing

A major criticism of the operational effectiveness of the investment reserve system, as used during the 1958-59 recession, related to its timing. It has been argued that better results could have been obtained if the reserve funds had been released six months earlier, i.e., in December, 1957, and discontinued at an earlier date. As it turned out, the maximum employment effect of the reserve was not felt until 15

---

[4] Curt Canarp, "Investment Reserves and How They Can Be Used to Combat Recession and Unemployment," *Quarterly Review of the Skandinaviska Banken,* April, 1963, p. 36.

[5] Permission to use the investment reserve funds was terminated in September, 1959. The economic upturn began in the summer of 1959. By 1960 special tax incentives were being offered to increase the amounts deposited in the Riksbank.

[6] The data excludes projects for which special government permits were needed, and forestry projects.

months after the permission for the release was granted by the Labor Market Board in May, 1958. By that time, the recession was over and the upturn was well under way.[7]

Curt Canarp, in an article in the Skandinaviska Banken, listed four criticisms of the release of the investment reserve funds in 1958-59:

1. The first was with respect to poor timing of the release of the funds.

2. There was some delay and indecisiveness on the part of the Labor Market Board to release the funds, attributable in part to a deficiency in economic forecasting.

3. There was an apparent breakdown in communications with the business sector involving the details of the release of the funds.

4. There was the feeling that the use of the reserve funds could have been directed in such a way that the labor market could have been affected more quickly.[8]

Two other criticisms have been made with respect to the use of the investment reserve as a device for economic stabilization:

1. The investment reserve benefits the large, well-established companies with a record of profit earnings, and has little meaning to companies with records of losses or marginal profits. As an economic stabilization device, its application would be uneven throughout the Swedish economy, both in boom periods when the objective might be to neutralize investment, and in a recession when the objective might be to stimulate investment. The smaller companies might well have had little or no investment funds to stimulate or neutralize for the reason that earnings could be considerably lower.

To a certain extent, this criticism has validity. However, there does not appear to be a one-sided concentration of the investment reserve in the larger companies. Swedish authorities in the Ministry of Finance and the Labor Market Board feel that the investment reserve is utilized by both large and small companies, and no changes have been made to favor one group over the other.

2. The investment reserve has had uneven effect throughout the Swedish economy. The release of the funds in 1958-59 and 1962-63 had an immediate effect in the industrial centers of the country—

---

[7] There is a fundamental dilemma of economic stabilization policy—the reconciliation of the long period of time which elapses between the decision to adopt a stabilization measure and its effect, and the short period of time in which changes in employment can be forecast with any degree of certainty.

[8] Canarp, *op. cit.*, p. 37.

Stockholm, Göteborg, Malmo, and Uppsala—but had little effect on employment in the small textile communities in the central and western parts of the country. Structural unemployment would be little affected by the release of the investment reserve.[9]

All economic stabilization devices—fiscal or monetary—have an uneven effect on a country's economy. Usually, the immediate objective is to stimulate or restrain overall aggregate demand. The 1964 tax cut in the United States was cast in the frame of reference of stimulating aggregate demand—a $10 billion reduction would result in an increase in GNP of approximately $25 billion, assuming that monetary policies are accommodating. However, fiscal and monetary devices have a very uneven impact among regions. An agricultural area, for example, would be less likely than an industrial area to be affected per dollar of potential GNP by a tax cut.[10]

In assessing the influence of the release of the investment reserve on investment and employment in the 1958-59 recession, it is apparent that the release stimulated employment—although belated—and also contributed in an important way to the increase in gross private domestic investment which occurred both in 1958 and in 1959. Gross private domestic investment in 1957 was 9.3 billion kronor; in 1958,

---

[9] The same criticism was levied at the U. S. tax cut of 1964. See, for example, the statement of Senator William Proxmire in the 1963 Joint Economic Report, pp. 40-42. Senator Proxmire states, "What good is a tax cut to an unemployed man with no income? He doesn't pay any taxes now. He doesn't need a tax cut. He needs a job."

[10] See Stanley Engerman, "Regional Aspects of Fiscal Federalism," in the book edited by Richard Musgrave, *Essays in Fiscal Federalism* (Washington: The Brookings Institution, 1966), pp. 7-63.

The Engerman essay pertains to the implication of fiscal policy from the standpoint of its effect on regional employment patterns. The premise in this essay is that general stabilization measures, i.e., tax reductions, have an uneven effect on the economy because differences exist in the economic structures of various regions. Fiscal policy as a stabilization device is normally concerned with national aggregates. A uniform fiscal effect throughout the economy is assumed when the effect of such fiscal measures as the 1964 tax cut is analyzed. Current statements pertaining to anti-inflationary tax policies also are presented in terms of the aggregative effect on the economy.

However, stabilization policies may have different effects on different economic regions. Regions in the United States are not homogeneous. A rural region in the south will have an entirely different employment pattern from that of a highly industrialized region in the east. Employment fluctuations vary regionally; therefore, general fiscal and monetary measures are bound to have dissimilar effects in different regions. Engerman concludes that to make stabilization policy effective, it is necessary to pinpoint specific measures for different regions. General fiscal and monetary policy measures must be complemented with specific measures—public works, relocation allowances— to insure a more effective stabilization policy.

10.2 billion kronor; and in 1959, 10.8 billion kronor. The manufacturing sector of gross private investment was 3.1 billion kronor in 1957; 3.5 billion kronor in 1958; and 3.7 billion in 1959.[11]

The Sterilization of the Investment Reserve in 1960-61

Normally, the restraining effect of the investment reserve during a boom period is minimal because the required deposit of 46 percent in the Riksbank is less than the effective tax rate of 49 percent. In other words, the setting aside of an investment reserve enhances slightly the liquidity of companies at a time when liquidity is not particularly desirable.

To restrict liquidity, the basic investment reserve provisions were changed in 1960 and 1961 to allow Swedish enterprises to obtain an additional deduction from taxable income provided that they deposited the full amount of the reserve (100 percent as opposed to 46 percent) in blocked accounts in the Riksbank during the tax year. As stated previously, in 1960 the tax deduction was an amount equal to 12 percent of the reserve payment if accomplished before August 1. If the deposit was made between August 1 and November 1, the tax deduction was 8 percent. In 1961, the same percentage applied to deposits before July 1 and October 1, respectively.

The sterilization of the entire reserve, or 100 percent reserve, had some effect on liquidity. There was a marked increase in the amount of new investment reserves registered over preceding years. Total new reserves registered in 1958 amounted to 419 million kronor; in 1959, 530 million kronor; and in 1960, 1,063 million kronor. The total amount of 100 percent reserves registered in 1960 amounted to 770 million kronor, and in 1961, 285 million kronor.[12]

The direct effect was to sterilize 770 million kronor out of the liquid funds of Swedish industrial firms for the latter part of 1960 and 285 million kronor out of liquid funds for the first half-year of 1961. This, in turn, served to reduce commercial bank liquidity, and also put a brake on the tendencies of the more liquid companies to

---

[11] National Central Bureau of Statistics, *National Accounts, 1950-65,* Stockholm: 1966, p. 24.

Gross private domestic investment in Swedish national income accounts is broken down into six categories: housing, manufacturing, power works, agriculture, communications, and other investment.

[12] The 770 million kronor were sterilized during the period from July to the end of 1960, and the 285 million kronor were sterilized from January to July of 1961.

lend to customers or to subcontractors.[13] The overall effect of the sterilization was also to put pressure on the level of interest rates upward.

One measure of the effect of 100 percent sterilization of the investment reserve is the liquidity ratio of Swedish commercial banks.[14] The liquidity ratio showed a decrease during the time that sterilization was in effect. The following table indicates changes in the liquidity ratio of the commercial banks.

TABLE IV. LIQUIDITY RATIOS FOR SWEDISH COMMERCIAL BANKS BY MONTHS, 1960-61

Months	1960	1961
January	48.7%	40.4%
February	49.8	41.3
March	45.7	37.6
April	44.4	37.7
May	42.3	34.3
June	41.2	35.9
July	38.7	37.1
August	39.2	38.7
September	37.6	34.6
October	40.9	38.6
November	38.1	37.7
December	41.1	41.2

Source: Sveriges Riksbank, Affarsbankernas Genomsnittliga Likviditet, Statistikkontoret, Stockholm, 1965

However, these changes in the liquidity ratio may be attributable only in part to the sterilization of the investment reserve. The Riksbank instituted stringent monetary policy measures, including a penalty rate over and above the official discount rate, to discourage borrowing on the part of the commercial banks.

Table V presents the net variations in blocked Riksbank investment reserve fund accounts for the 1960-61 period.

---

[13] To a certain extent, the effect is similar to Federal Reserve open-market operations.

[14] The liquidity ratio for Swedish commercial banks is obtained by dividing net claims on the Riksbank, claims on the National Debt Office and on other commercial banks, and housing bonds, by demand deposits (all deposits).

TABLE V. NET VARIATIONS IN BLOCKED RIKSBANK INVESTMENT
RESERVE ACCOUNTS, 1960-61

(Millions of kronor)

	Net Variations in Blocked Investment Reserve Accounts
1960	
First Quarter	+ 75
Second Quarter	+ 40
Third Quarter	+543
Fourth Quarter	+203
Total	+863
1961	
First Quarter	+ 58
Second Quarter	+242
Third Quarter	+ 65
Fourth Quarter	—279
Total	+ 86

Source: Sveriges Riksbank (Annual Reports of the Central Bank of Sweden for 1960 and 1961).

As can be seen in the above table, nearly three quarters of a billion kronor were shifted into blocked Riksbank accounts during the last two quarters of 1960. In the second quarter of 1961, a quarter of a billion kronor were shifted into blocked accounts. The large shifts out of corporate accounts in the commercial banks into blocked accounts in the Riksbank placed a substantial strain on the lending capacity of the commercial banking system. This fact is reflected in the liquidity ratio table (Table IV). Liquid assets in the Swedish commercial banks declined by 808 million kronor in 1960. In the first and second quarters of 1961, liquid assets of the commercial banks declined by 1.4 billion kronor.[15]

In 1960 the Swedish government levied for the first time a general turnover tax (omsättningsskatt). The yield to the government from this new revenue source amounted to 1.1 billion kronor for 1960, and 1.6 billion kronor for 1961. Total tax revenues to the government from all indirect taxes—automobile duties, tobacco taxes, the general

---

[15] Sveriges Riksbank (Annual Reports of Central Bank of Sweden for 1960 and 1961).

purchase tax, taxes on alcohol, and other indirect taxes—increased from 5.4 billion kronor in 1959 to 7.6 billion kronor in 1962.

Revisions in the personal income tax also increased the amount of revenue from direct taxes. In 1959 total tax revenue to the Swedish government from direct taxation amounted to 7.1 billion kronor, in 1960, 7.8 billion kronor, and in 1961, 9.3 billion kronor.

As an anti-inflationary measure, sterilization of the investment reserve had some effect on the price level through a reduction in the lending potential of the Swedish commercial banks. Also a considerable volume of funds, which might have been invested, were neutralized. However, the specific effect is very difficult to measure. As mentioned previously, Swedish monetary policy was switched to a restrictive direction. During 1960, the Swedish government introduced a turnover tax which, in itself, was bound to exert some effect on the economy.

Gross private domestic investment increased at an accelerated rate over previous years. In 1960, gross private domestic investment amounted to 12.5 billion kronor, an increase of 17 percent over the preceding year. In 1961, gross private domestic investment amounted to 14.2 billion kronor. Direct investment in manufacturing amounted to 4.5 billion kronor in 1960—a 20 percent increase over the preceding year, and 5.5 billion in 1961.

Sterilization of over one billion kronor in investment reserve funds undoubtedly reduced the level of investment in 1960 and 1961. No one knows to what extent, and it is significant to note that in 1963 when the investment reserve system was changed by parliament to include release of the funds for the purpose of encouraging the location of industry in northern Sweden,[16] it was recommended by a study commission that 100 percent sterilization of the investment reserves not be made a permanent part of the system.[17]

The Release of the Reserves in 1962-63

Unemployment in the pulp and paper and building construction industries led to the second release of the investment reserves. Per-

[16] This change created problems and was dropped in 1965.

[17] When questioned by the author why the investment reserves had not been sterilized in 1965, when the price level rose by 9 percent, or in 1966, when it also rose, officials of the Riksbank and Labor Market Board were of the opinion that:

(1) no clear-cut evidence was available to show that sterilization in 1960 and 1961 had an anti-inflationary effect; and

(2) general monetary measures instituted by the Riksbank would accomplish as much without having to pay the price of the inducements for sterilization.

mission to use the investment reserves was first given to the pulp and paper industry in December, 1961. In May, 1962, the Labor Market Board, concerned about an expected substantial increase in unemployment in building construction for the fall and winter months, authorized a general release of investment reserves for building projects. These projects had to begin before November, 1962, and the reserves were available for projects carried out during the time period July, 1962, to April, 1963. In this way the maximum effect on employment was produced during the winter months when unemployment in building construction is at its highest.

By the latter part of 1962, the recession had spread to the metal and machine tool industry. Orders were falling off and unemployment occurred. The Labor Market Board and the Ministry of Finance decided in November of 1962 to authorize the use of investment reserves for machinery investments.[18] Permission was given to use the reserves for this purpose. Orders had to be placed before May, 1963. Through March, 1963, permits to use investment reserves for machinery investments amounted to 280 million kronor ($54,000,-000.)[19] Coupled with this release of investment reserves was a speed-up of state and local government orders to the metal and machine tool industry.

Industrial plant construction, however, was the sector of investment on which the release of investment reserves had the greatest employment-creating effect. For example, in August of 1962, the total number of workers employed in plant construction amounted to 28,560; of this number, 1,600 workers or 6 percent were employed on projects using investment reserves. In November, 1962, the total work force had increased to 34,860; however, of this total, 8,500 workers or 24.5 percent were employed on projects using investment reserves. In February of 1963, 10,100 workers or 31 percent of all workers were employed on investment reserve projects.[20]

Timing

The timing of the release of the investment reserves during the 1962-63 recession was far superior to the timing in the 1958-59 recession. The county offices of the Labor Market Board had noted an

[18] The Ministry of Finance is responsible for general economic policy; the Labor Market Board is responsible for its implementation.
[19] The great majority of this amount went for purchases of machinery and equipment from the shipbuilding, metal, and machine tool industries.
[20] Canarp, *op. cit.,* p. 38.

increase in anticipated layoffs by industrial firms late in 1961 and early in 1962. Investment surveys taken in October, 1961, and March, 1962, by the Labor Market Board also indicated a decline in planned industrial investment.

Early in 1962 the county offices of the Labor Market Board contacted business firms possessing investment reserve funds and indicated that a release of the funds was imminent. In May, 1962, the release of reserve funds for construction was announced. It was stipulated that projects be started before November 1, for the reason that a substantial increase in construction activity was needed during the winter months when unemployment in the construction industry is normally quite high.

Unemployment rates for the time period involved are presented below. They reflect the downturn in business activity which was noted during the latter part of 1961 and the early part of 1962.

TABLE VI. UNEMPLOYMENT RATES, BY MONTHS, FOR SWEDEN, 1961-63

(In percent)

Year	Jan.	Feb.	Mar.	Apr.	May	June	July	Aug.	Sept.	Oct.	Nov.	Dec.
1961	2.1	2.0	1.5	1.6	1.1	.7	.5	.7	.7	.9	1.2	1.4
1962	2.1	2.2	2.0	1.8	1.3	.8	.6	.8	.8	1.0	1.2	1.3
1963	3.6	2.5	1.9	1.8	1.1	.7	.6	.8	.9	1.1	1.3	1.5

Source: Sammanstallning Arbetsmarknadstabeller, Kungl Arbetsmarknadsstyrelsen, Stockholm, January, 1964.

Employment Effect

The release of the reserve funds had a more immediate effect on employment than the earlier release. The effect can be summarized in the following table.

Gunnar Eliasson, in his study of the operation of the investment reserves in the 1962-63 recession, makes several main points.[21] The geographical distribution of the net effects of the release of the investment reserve was not particularly favorable. The impact of the release was concentrated in the larger industrial areas where unemployment was not a serious problem, and an acute labor shortage actually existed for many types of skilled workers. Rural areas in

---

[21] Gunnar Eliasson, *Investment Funds in Operation*, National Institute of Economic Research, Stockholm, 1965. His study is first-rate and this chapter relies upon his findings.

TABLE VII. TOTAL EMPLOYMENT EFFECT ON INVESTMENT
RESERVE FINANCED PROJECTS

Years and Months	Total Employment Effect [1]
1962	
August	1,300
November	8,200
1963	
February	10,200
May	8,200
August	5,700

[1] This refers to employment on construction projects only. In November, 1962, funds were released for investment in machinery and equipment. Employment created as a result of increased orders for machinery and equipment is not reflected in the employment total.

Source: Data furnished by the Labor Market Board at the request of the author.

northern Sweden, where unemployment has been well above the national average for the last decade, were affected only moderately by the release. Most of the investment that occurred was in the expanding industrial regions of central and southern Sweden, a fact which is amplified by the following table:

TABLE VIII. INVESTMENT RESERVE PROJECTS BY REGIONS

Region	Number of Projects
Far North	37
Dalarna and southern Norrland	90
Metropolitan area and county of Stockholm	64
Other Mälar counties	148
East Götaland	160
Skäne, Halland, and Blekinge	148
West Coast and Vänar counties	211
Total	858

Source: Gunnar Eliasson, "Investment Funds in Operation," National Institute of Economic Research, Stockholm, 1965, p. 96.

The only way to circumvent this concentration is to screen investment reserve projects in favor of the areas with the highest unemployment rates. This, however, converts the investment reserve from a short-run stabilization device into a device which attempts to influence the location of industry. From 1963 to 1965, the Swedes used the investment reserve as an inducement to get firms to locate in depressed areas; however, the approach was dropped for the reason that it was not consistent with the basic objective of the reserve.

The net employment effect, according to Eliasson, also varied considerably by regions.[22] Table IX illustrates this point.

TABLE IX. EMPLOYMENT EFFECTS OF THE INVESTMENT RESERVE BY REGIONS

Region	Average Number of Workers in the Construction Sector During Periods of Release	Average Net Effect During Period of Release, Number of Workers	Net Effect As a Percentage of Unemployment
Far North	9,190	130	1.4%
Dalarna and southern Norrland	12,230	540	4.4
Metropolitan area and Stockholm	19,290	440	2.3
Other Mälar counties	12,700	730	5.7
East Götaland	11,860	540	4.6
Skåne, Halland and Blekinge	13,290	490	3.7
West Coast and Väner counties	18,340	1,080	5.9
Total	96,900	3,940	4.1

Source: Gunnar Eliasson, "Investment Funds in Operation," National Institute of Economic Research, Stockholm, 1965, p. 96.

The Far North and Dalarna and southern Norrland have 70 percent of the land area of Sweden, but only 20 percent of the population. Both regions are predominantly rural (agriculture and forestry) and possess the highest unemployment rates in Sweden. The West-Coast and Vaner region is also rural in composition and has had above-average unemployment rates.

Eliasson also shows that the monetary effect of the release of the reserves also varied considerably by regions.[23] The regions with the highest unemployment rates, the Far North, received less of a stimulus from the release of the reserves than other regions. Table X illustrates this point.

Eliasson found that as far as a release of investment reserve funds was concerned, a powerful impact of short duration could be secured at short notice.[24] The time lag between the announcement of the release of the funds and their initial effect on investment was small.

[22] *Ibid.*, pp. 88-96.
[23] *Ibid.*, pp. 89-90.
[24] *Ibid.*, p. 67.

TABLE X. MONETARY EFFECT OF THE RELEASE OF THE
RESERVES BY REGIONS

Region	Total Industrial Investment During Period of Release (millions of kronor)	Total Investment Reserve During Period of Release (millions of kronor)	Reserves as a Percentage of Total Industrial Investment
Far North	136	29	21%
Dalarna and southern Norrland	152	71	47
Metropolitan area and county of Stockholm	180	63	35
Other Mälar counties	198	77	39
East Götaland	101	60	59
Skäne, Halland, and Blekinge	194	66	34
West Coast and Väner counties	267	110	41
Total	1,228	476	39

Source: Gunnar Eliasson, "Investment Funds in Operation," National Institute of Economic Research, Stockholm, 1965, p. 96.

The announcement took place in early May of 1962, and by September a substantial net increase in industrial construction had taken place. The maximum impact of the release of the funds took place in February of 1963—less than a year after the announcement of release. By May of 1963, the impact had tapered off considerably. The bulk of the investment effect took place during the winter months of 1962-63, during which a decline in investment activity in the construction sector had been forecast. For the whole period of release—July 1, 1962 to April 30, 1963—Eliasson calculated a net positive impact on construction activity of no less than 300 million kronor, or an average of 30 million kronor per month.

During the 1962-63 recession, the Central Bank of Sweden pursued an easy money policy. The discount rate, which had been raised to 5 percent during the 1960 boom period, was lowered to 4 percent in the fall of 1962, and 3.5 percent in January of 1963. The average discount rate for three months' Treasury bills, which had been 5 percent in 1960, was lowered to 3.8 percent in the winter of 1963. Total commercial bank lending to the public increased by 400 million kronor during the recession, reflecting the more liberal monetary policy followed by the Central Bank.[25]

Expenditures by the Swedish government on public works, housing

[25] Sveriges Riksbank, Annual Reports for 1962 and 1963.

construction, and placement of government orders to industry also increased during the recession. Total expenditures on public works construction amounted to 380 million kronor during the fiscal year 1962-63. In the winter months of 1963, an average of 13,000 workers were employed on public works projects. In January and February of 1963, government orders for machinery were increased to forestall decline in employment caused by a reduction in exports. The Labor Market Board also extended subsidies to counties and municipalities covering 20 percent of the orders for machinery and equipment placed by them over and above their previously established purchasing programs. Housing construction was also used as an employment-creating device during the 1962-63 recession. More than 90 percent of total housing production in Sweden is financed with government loans, and employment in the building industry can easily be influenced by the easing or tightening of housing credit. In the 1962-63 recession, increased housing construction, together with the release of private industry's countercyclical reserve funds, created approximately 10,000 jobs in building construction out of a total of some 50,000 jobs that were created by all of the employment programs.[26]

A basic requisite for the effective operation of the investment reserve is good short-run forecasting. Evidence shows that forecasting techniques had been improved considerably over 1958. More frequent surveys of investment intentions of business firms by the Labor Market Board, and labor market surveys of employment taken in each county, have expedited forecasting. There was a sharp improvement in the timing of the release of the reserve funds due in part to better forecasting in the 1962-63 recession over the release in the 1958-59 recession. This meant that more investment was undertaken during the period when it was needed, and less was being carried out after the recession had ended. Nevertheless, forecasting of employment prospects cannot be made with any degree of certainty for much more than six months in the future, and decisions to invest and the physical execution of investment involve a considerable time lag. To be effective, economic stabilization policy needs improved forecasting techniques and advanced planning of investment.

At the Stockholm School of Economics, Professor Sven-Erik Johansson has investigated the effect of the use of investment reserves

---

[26] Martin Schnitzer, "Unemployment Programs in Sweden," Joint Economic Committee of the U. S. Congress, 88th Congress, 2d Session, 1964, pp. 44-48.

on the investment planning of companies which utilized their investment reserves in 1962-63.[27] The objective was to find out to what extent permits were granted for investment which would have been carried out during the same period anyway. The answer is crucial to an evaluation of the effectiveness of the investment reserve system.

The results of the study are summarized as follows:

1. Half of the companies interviewed reported that the investment reserves were used for investments that would have been carried out during the same period anyway. The investment reserve funds returned by the Riksbank had no noticeable effect in terms of additional investment. The reasons were either that the companies had a satisfactory liquid position or the additional funds were of a relatively small size.[28]

2. About half of the companies indicated that the investments for which the investment reserves were used, were carried out at an earlier date than they otherwise would have been.

Apparently, the main effect of the permission to use the investment reserve, at least as far as the companies that were used in the sample were concerned, was in relation to timing. Eleven out of 23 companies indicated that a change in investment plans occurred as a result of permission to use the investment reserve. Six of the 11 companies reported that investments were started anywhere from three months to a year earlier than planned; the remaining five indicated that plans to invest had been moved up a year or more when permission to use the reserves was granted. One company in the sample reported that investment would not have been carried out without the investment reserves.[29]

Although it is dangerous to generalize, two points can be made with reference to the above study and to business decisions to invest in general. First, as indicated in the study, release of the reserve does prompt some business firms to invest earlier than anticipated—a "plus" factor in a recession; and, second, the use of the reserve with its attendant tax benefits, probably would not be a key factor in investment decisions. In other words, it is quite likely that many Swedish firms would have invested in buildings and capital goods, with or

---

[27] Sven-Erik Johansson, "An Appraisal of the Swedish System of Investment Reserves," *The International Journal of Accounting,* Vol. 1, No. 1, Fall, 1965, pp. 85-92.

[28] *Ibid.,* p. 90.

[29] Data furnished to the author by Professor Johansson.

without the use of the investment reserve. In this connection, it should be pointed out that anti-recessionary measures as used by the Swedish government are quite comprehensive, and include increases in public works construction, granting of more permits to build housing (a short commodity in the Swedish cities), and increases in government purchases from industry. General monetary measures—easier credit, lower interest rates—also come into play.

Conclusion

To encourage Swedish firms to take measures calculated to even out business fluctuations, Swedish law provides that they may set aside a certain portion of their profits for future investment free of the income tax. These reserves must be deposited either in a fund for industry or a fund for forestry, but 46 percent of the amount deposited must be placed in a special blocked account in the national bank. These deposits are under the supervision of the National Labor Market Board, and can be used only under certain conditions and for purposes prescribed by law. Special tax concessions are granted to business firms that utilize the investment reserve fund.

The investment reserve funds were released during the 1958-59 recession. A total of one billion kronor was used for housing construction, roads, forestry, machinery, and equipment. From the standpoint of creating employment, at least in the construction industry, the release of the funds had a propitious effect. However, from the standpoint of timing, a conspicuous failure was recorded. The funds were released well after the recession was underway, and the effect on the economy was felt almost a year after the start of the recession. Most of the expenditures took place during the upswing, and the cumulative effects were still being felt during the boom period of 1960.

The investment reserve was used as an anti-inflationary device in 1960-61. Additional tax incentives were used to induce the full amount (100 percent) of the investment reserves into the Bank of Sweden. The results were considered mixed. There is evidence to show that the liquidity positions of the commercial banks were reduced sharply during the period 1960-61. However, a stringent monetary policy was pursued at the same time by the Bank of Sweden.

The investment reserve funds were released again during the 1962-63 recession. From the standpoint of timing, the release of of the funds was more effective than the release in the 1958-59 recession. The employment-creating effects of the release were also greater than in 1958-59.

The operation of the investment reserve system can be summarized as follows:

1. The release of the reserves had a stimulating effect on investment and employment in both recessions;

2. The restraining effect of the reserves during an inflation is less pronounced because the required deposit of 46 percent is less than the effective tax rate of 49 percent, i.e., allocations to the reserve system enhance the liquidity of firms at a time when liquidity is not a basic desideratum;

3. Compared to other devices used to stimulate investment— depreciation allowances and investment deductions—the investment reserve has two advantages: flexibility, in that the Labor Market Board can authorize its use for all sectors of the economy or a particular sector, and, the fact that allocations to the reserve maintain an option on future tax deductions, i.e., in order to realize such gains, firms must be prepared to invest during periods when the reserves may be used;

4. The reserve system acts as an incentive to well managed, highly liquid firms to conform to the nation's desire to maintain full employment, and at the same time avoids governmental administrative burdens connected with the support of individual projects; and

5. Although there is an element of subsidy in the form of tax allowances, the intention of providing the reserve system is not to subsidize or protect weak or badly managed firms.

One might wonder, however, whether it would not be fairer and simpler to give firms an outright subsidy to invest during a recession instead of relying on the investment reserve.[30] For example, the government could agree to pay 50 percent of the cost of all investments above a certain percentage of a firm's average investment level over the last five years. This approach might well be superior to the present investment reserve system in the cost to the government per unit of investment since firms would be compelled to in-

---

[30] This point has been made by Lars C. Sandberg in his comment on the article by Erwin Mildner and Ira Scott, "An Innovation in Fiscal Policy: The Swedish Investment Reserve," *National Tax Journal,* September, 1962, pp. 280-83; Lundberg's, A Comment on "An Innovation in Fiscal Policy: The Swedish Investment Reserve System," appears in the *National Tax Journal,* March, 1963, pp. 107-08.

44

crease investment above the average level in order to take advantage of the subsidy.[31] The direct subsidy would cover more companies than the investment reserve, since the latter is limited to those companies that make formal deposits to reserves.

---

[31] *Ibid.,* p. 108.

THE INVESTMENT TAX

Introduction

A second Swedish anti-inflationary device is a direct tax on investment. It was used several times in the decade of the 1950s when inflationary pressures were prevalent in the Swedish economy. The tax amounted to a rate of 10 to 12 percent on capital expenditures. The tax was in effect in 1951 and 1952 but was withdrawn for 1953 and 1954. It was again applied on an annual basis in 1955, 1956, and 1957. The tax was not renewed in 1958 and has not been used since.

The Application of the Tax

The investment tax was a temporary tax on certain capital expenditures, in particular expenditures for machinery and equipment, new or used, with an anticipated life of more than three years, and expenditures for new buildings, or for the remodeling, rebuilding, or expansion of existing buildings. The tax also applied to the repair and maintenance of existing buildings; however, a deduction of 2 percent of the assessed value of the property was allowed for ordinary upkeep and maintenance. The tax did not apply to the purchase of used buildings. The repair or replacement of property damaged or destroyed by fire and other phenomena was not taxable to the extent that the cost did not exceed more than 200 percent of the insurance recovery. Expenditures for the development of mineral resources were subject to the tax, unless deductible as current operating expenses. The tax was not applicable to increases in inventories.[1]

---

[1] World Tax Series, *Taxation in Sweden* (Boston: Little, Brown and Co., 1959), pp. 157-61. The chapter relies heavily on this tax series to provide the details of the investment tax.

The investment tax was a flat tax levied on the sum total of the taxpayer's taxable investment for the year less an exemption which for 1956 amounted to 20,000 kronor, and for 1957, 30,000 kronor.[2] The tax rates for 1957, the last year the tax was used, was 12 percent. The tax was deductible for purposes of both the national and local income taxes; the effect being to reduce the impact of the tax considerably.[3]

Certain expenditures were specifically exempted from the investment tax:

1. Expenditures on rolling stock.
2. Expenditures for housing.
3. Expenditures on oil storage facilities with a capacity of at least 1,000 cubic meters.
4. Expenditures for buses for commercial purposes.
5. Expenditures for commercial or fishing vessels with a gross weight under 100 tons.
6. Investments in facilities for the production or distribution of electric power.
7. Investment in branch offices or the construction of facilities in other countries.
8. Expenditures for military preparedness.

The Evaluation of the Investment Tax

The investment tax was designed as an anti-inflation rather than a revenue measure. It was levied directly on the value of new investments in an effort to keep capital investment within the limits of available resources. It attempted to cause a leveling out in the business cycle by penalizing investment expenditures in periods of high economic activity, thus causing a postponement of at least some investment to periods when slack economic conditions would make such expenditures desirable from the standpoint of employment.

The investment tax is an extra burden on the investments of business firms and may be placed in the category of taxation on expenditures. The imposition of the tax on a business firm entails a

---

[2] The tax applied to any person subject to the national income tax who made taxable investments in connection with one of three categories of property—agricultural (including forestry), real, and business.

[3] The tax was labeled a "special" tax, and "special" Swedish taxes are deducted from business income. "Special" taxes are regarded as costs of carrying on a business, which bear on particular transactions.

worsening of its liquidity and its profit earning capacity. The worsening of liquidity, however, is offset to a degree when the tax is deductible as an operating cost for the purpose of assessment of the national income tax.

Investment expenditures are one of four major components of aggregate demand.[4] However, from the standpoint of economic stabilization, investment expenditures create several problems: Firstly, investment expenditures have an impact on an economy's productive capacity in that they are made for the acquisition of capital goods, whose sole purpose is to produce other goods and services. The productive capacity of an economy is largely determined by the rate of investment. Secondly, investment expenditures, especially on inventories, are considered to be the most volatile of the aggregate demand components. There are greater fluctuations in expenditures on capital goods than on consumer goods. Volatility in investment expenditures will have an impact on income, employment, and the business cycle. It is this volatility that the investment tax, (and for that matter, the investment reserve also) attempts to diminish.

It is possible to be certain of the direction in which the investment tax will work. The imposition of the tax is tantamount to an increase in costs. Marginal, or less profitable investment, will not be carried out. Dividend pay-out policies would be affected to the extent that a firm would have to secure a higher yield from its investment to maintain its same dividends, or else reduce its dividends. The imposition of the tax will cause some investment to be postponed to a more desirable time.

If, however, the investment tax is to have full effect, it must be a temporary one and not made permanent. For an effect designed to postpone investment must always be stronger than one that definitely aims at putting a brake on investment. If firms have reason to believe that the investment tax will be imposed for a long time ahead, they will soon adapt their estimates of earning capacity, and their financing plans accordingly. Perhaps only the least profitable investments will be abandoned. If, on the other hand, firms know that the tax is

---

[4] As a result of theoretical developments stemming from the work of Keynes and of advances in the field of national income accounting, it is possible to identify the four major components of an economy's aggregate demand structure: consumption, investment, government purchases of goods and services, and the export-import balance. The components fit into the familiar and fundamental identity equation,

$Y = C + I + G + X - M$, where $Y =$ national income, $C =$ consumption, $I =$ investment, $G =$ government expenditures, $X =$ exports and $M =$ imports.

only temporary, it is likely that even more essential and profitable investments can be postponed for a year or so.

Erik Lundberg wrote as follows in 1955 with regard to the investment taxes of 1953 and 1955.

> The investment tax as a method of curtailing investments has been considered in Sweden to be preferable in many cases to a raising of the rate of interest. The tax can discriminate between different kinds of investments, and the increased cost of investment does not involve any increase in private incomes as an increase of investment rates may. But a great deal of uncertainty surrounds the actual effects on prices and demands of these investment taxes. The effects will be influenced, e.g., by speculation in the duration of the tax. Swedish experiences do not allow any definite conclusions to be made. So many other factors were at work during these years that statistical analysis of the effects of the investment tax is impossible.[5]

How far the investment tax was effective as an anti-inflationary device is not clear. However, three different viewpoints may be presented:

1. It was argued that the investment tax contributed to inflation by reducing investment that might have led to increased production and hence to a lessening of inflation.[6] The proper objective should be to increase the productive capacity of the economy, not decrease it. An increase in the supply of capital goods, or any measure that would result in plant modernization or improved productive capacity, would increase the outflow of goods and services to offset increases in aggregate demand.[7] This can be presented in the following diagram:

---

[5] Erik Lundberg, *Business Cycles and Economic Policy* (Cambridge: Harvard University Press, 1957), p. 217.

[6] This argument can also be made with respect to the suspension of the investment credit in the U. S. See the hearings before the House Ways and Means Committee on the suspension of the investment credit.

[7] With full employment of all resources a logical concomitant of inflation, the question arises—how can the supply of capital goods increase when all available resources are being utilized? Increased investment will place further strains on existing resources. However, plant modernization and improved technology brought about by investment could very well result in increased output with fixed resources. Capital may be substituted for labor, and industries, as they become more capital intensive, are capable of greater output.

However, this argument is more applicable in the long run. In the short run, with resources fixed, an investment results in increased competition with

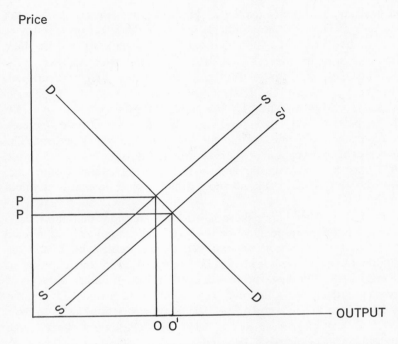

In the diagram, the price level is represented on the vertical axis, and output is represented on the horizontal axis. The original price level is represented by the symbol P and original output by the symbol O. Inflation is assumed to exist. Increasing investment, rather than decreasing it would increase the supply of capital goods, which, in turn, would increase the supply of goods and services. The supply curve, S, shifts to the right, S', with the result that output increases and the price level falls.

2. It has been argued that so many factors were at work during the impositions of the investment tax that an exact conclusion is impossible. For example, under the 1955 amendments to the 1938 tax law that introduced the investment reserve, free depreciation was eliminated.[8] This elimination was bound to have had some effect

---

the consumer and public sectors of the economy for scarce resources. The result is usually a rise in prices.

The investment tax would be more effective if demand-pull inflation exists. The appropriate remedy is to decrease one of the components of aggregate demand. If cost-push inflation exists, the investment tax probably would be ineffective.

[8] Free depreciation refers to the right of business firms to write off machinery and equipment as they see fit. Regardless of the anticipated life of a

on investment in 1956 and 1957, years in which the investment tax was levied. Therefore, it is difficult to isolate the effect on investment that resulted from the elimination of free depreciation from the effect that was brought about by the levying of the investment tax.

Monetary policy effects also have to be taken into consideration. The discount rate of the Riksbank was raised in April, 1955, by 1 percent to 3¾ percent. In November, 1956, a second increase of ¼ percent was made and in July of 1957 a third increase of 1 percent was made, so that the discount rate was 5 percent. The most important weapon of monetary policy during 1955, 1956, and 1957 was, however, the direct restrictions on advances. From June, 1955, to July, 1957, bank advances declined by 5 percent in nominal value.

3. On the other hand, there is evidence to show that the investment tax did have some effect on the Swedish economy. The combined effects of the credit squeeze imposed by the central bank and the investment tax (levied from the beginning of 1955 and expiring at the end of 1957) have been estimated in two separate surveys of investment decisions to amount to a reduction of planned investment by 14 percent in 1955 and 1956. The credit restrictions seem to have been the most effective measure, while the deflationary effect of the investment tax declined in 1956 compared to 1955.[9]

There is also an indication that the investment tax was at least partly effective in postponing capital expenditures to a time when inflationary pressures had diminished. Industrial investment in Sweden went up by about 10 percent in 1958 over the amount of investment in 1957.[10]

The Joint Economic Committee of the U. S. Congress, in its report, "Economic Policy for Western Europe," concludes that the elimination of the investment tax for 1958, in addition to other measures taken at the same time, contributed to an expansion of

---

machine, its entire cost could be written off in the year of acquisition. Between 1938 and 1955, Swedish corporations and economic associations were allowed free depreciation of machinery and equipment—the right to write off the cost of any piece of machinery or equipment completely in the year of acquisition, or on any other basis deemed appropriate.

It was argued that free depreciation contributed to postwar inflation in Sweden, particularly in the early 1950s, for the reason that business firms were induced to make investments to acquire depreciable objects at the very time that investment required restriction rather than stimulation.

[9] Konjunktur Läget Hosten 1957, Meddelanden Frän Konjunkturinstutet, Stockholm: 1957, p. 68.

[10] National Central Bureau of Statistics, *National Income Accounts, 1950-1965*, Stockholm, 1966.

private investment expenditures in 1958 approximately twice as great, in money terms, as that in the public sector.[11]

Although the tax was used as an anti-inflationary measure, the revenue produced was considerable. In 1957 the tax raised 201,699,-600 kronor ($39 million) based on total taxable expenditures of 1,681 million kronor ($300 million). In 1956 the tax yielded 87 million kronor on taxable investment expenditures of 727 million kronor.

The investment tax was discontinued in 1958 and has not been used since. There are several reasons for this:

1. In 1960 Swedish industrial investments became subject to a general purchase tax. The tax represents a substantial source of income to the Swedish government and, in fact, was not suspended during the 1962-63 recessions. There is a consensus of opinion among Swedish fiscal experts that the general purchase tax itself has a certain anti-inflationary bias, and that to superimpose the investment tax over and above the purchase tax would be a mistake.

2. There is the feeling among some Swedish fiscal experts that the investment tax had an uneven effect on investment in that it penalized the larger and more efficient firms while leaving the inefficient firms untouched. The tax, it was felt, adversely affected Sweden's balance of payments because of the effect on the export-oriented automobile and steel industries.

3. The investment reserve fund was used as a countercyclical fiscal instrument in the 1958-59 recession, again in the boom period of 1960-61, and for a third time in the recession of 1962-63. The investment reserve possesses a greater degree of flexibility than the investment tax in that it can be applied to specific industries or to industries in general. The investment reserve can also be used as an instrument of localization policy.[12] The investment reserve, then, has supplanted the investment tax as an instrument of economic stabilization.

---

[11] Joint Economic Committee, "Economic Policy in Western Europe," U. S. Congress, 85th Congress, 2d Session, 1959, p. 37.

[12] In July, 1963, the Swedish government announced its decision to authorize the release of investment reserve funds for the purpose of encouraging the location of industry in the four northernmost provinces in Sweden, and some areas of central Sweden. These areas have had the highest unemployment rate in Sweden.

Investment reserve funds for industry as well as forestry were allowed to be used for projects started in these areas. Companies located within the depressed areas, as well as those located outside, were allowed to use the funds.

The policy, however, was discontinued in 1965.

4. A disadvantage of the investment tax, even though it may be temporary in nature, is that it invariably cannot achieve the full effect intended for the reason that business firms usually have made their plans and resolved upon their investments far in advance. The investment is frequently of such a nature that it is impossible to upset the plan without serious difficulty. In that case, the investment tax does not have the intended effect of postponing the investment.

Conclusion

The investment tax was used on several occasions during the 1950s. It was a flat tax of 10 or 12 percent on all investment carried out during a given year, less certain exemptions. The tax was used as an anti-inflationary measure, but opinions differ on the extent of its effectiveness. However, the investment tax was effective in that some investment that probably would have taken place during the time period in which the tax was imposed was postponed until a later time period. Evidence exists to support this point. Since the tax was temporary, Swedish firms postponed some investment in anticipation of the lifting of the tax. Investment in 1958 increased approximately 10 percent over 1957—the last year that the investment tax was in effect.

However, in 1958 the investment reserve was utilized for the first time as a countercyclical instrument. Amendments in 1955 to the original law had made it more attractive for business firms to place a part of their earnings in an investment reserve. Total investment reserve funds in that economy had been increased considerably by 1958. Reliance, then, was placed on the investment reserve.

In 1960 a purchase tax was levied on industrial purchases. This tax, to a certain extent, has the same effect as the investment tax, although its object is to provide revenue for the Swedish government. The use of the purchase tax (it is still in use) means that the investment tax is no longer as desirable or feasible as it was back in the last decade.

CONCLUSIONS

One of the main sources of economic growth is investment. Investment is required, not only to increase the total stock of equipment and buildings, but also to allow labor to be employed on increasingly productive jobs as old plant and machinery is replaced by new. However, investment is the most unstable component of aggregate demand, and economists have long been interested in measures that would stabilize investment practices.

The Swedish government has attempted to influence the timing of private investment projects through special tax concessions to firms which are willing to postpone their particular investment projects, so as to fit them into a more stable general pattern. The device used is the investment reserve fund—a system where firms are allowed to make tax-free allocations of profits to a special fund which is to be used for investment during a recession. Tax concessions also accrue to the firm that uses the funds during the prescribed time.

The investment reserve funds were released on two occasions—the 1958-59 and 1962-63 recessions—and the results were mixed. As far as the employment-creating effects were concerned, the releases did provide additional employment, particularly in the construction industry. In the 1958-59 recession, permits were granted to more than 600 firms to use investment reserves of 700 million Swedish kronor. Together with special permits granted by the government, a total of more than one billion kronor was released. This amount corresponded to approximately one-fifth of total private industrial investment in one year.

In the 1962-63 recession, permission was given by the Labor Market Board to business firms to draw on the investment reserve funds for building construction. Projects had to be started before

November 1, 1962. Moreover, the reserves could only be used for capital expenditures incurred before May 1, 1963. Permits were given to 554 companies to utilize approximately 700 million kronor.

On November 30, 1962, the Labor Market Board also authorized the use of investment reserve funds to be utilized for investment in machinery and other equipment intended for regular use. There had been a decline in the flow of incoming orders to the engineering industry, including shipyards, in 1962. Orders for machinery and equipment had to be placed before May 1, 1963, and deliveries were to be made by a date within the year that would hopefully have a desired effect on employment. Approximately 300 million kronor of investment reserve funds were utilized for investment in machinery and equipment. The greatest percentage of these funds was utilized by engineering and shipyard industries. Government purchases from the shipyards also increased by some 30 million kronor during 1963.

However, extenuating circumstances make it impossible to assign the investment reserve a high rating as a countercyclical fiscal instrument. First of all, it is uncertain as to how effective it would be in the absence of a number of other programs which are used by the Swedish government—public works, government orders to industry, increases in housing construction, and relocation of unemployed workers. General fiscal and monetary policy measures are also used. It is difficult to isolate the effects of the investment reserve from the overall effects of stabilization policies in general.

Secondly, the operational effectiveness of the program has been tried during a period of relatively high levels of economic activity within Sweden and in the other Scandinavian countries. The unemployment rate, even during the worst months of both recessions was low by American standards. Most of the unemployment that existed was either seasonal or structural in nature, and was limited primarily to the rural areas. One might legitimately question the effectiveness of the investment reserve, given an unemployment rate of 5 or 6 percent, or given a sharp decline in exports. Would business firms be as willing to invest if faced with a decline in export markets or a serious increase in unemployment?

It is also evident that the investment reserve program has a definite capital bias, and its effectiveness is uncertain, particularly with respect to less industrialized rural areas characterized by a surplus of labor resources. The capital-oriented industries benefit more from the release of the investment reserve than labor-oriented industries. Industries using skilled labor—the type that is least likely to be unemployed—are more likely to use the reserve, than industries using semi-skilled and unskilled labor.

It has been argued that larger firms are more likely to benefit from the investment reserve system than smaller firms. The larger firms usually have ample liquid assets and, during a boom, can continue their investment activity and, at the same time, take advantage of the investment reserve facilities. There is little evidence, however, to support the notion that the investment reserves are the exclusive domain of the larger Swedish firms.

The effectiveness of the investment reserve system depends on the extent to which it can stimulate a volume of investment which is in excess of that which would have been made in any case. Unquestionably, a considerable volume of investment would have taken place with or without the release of the reserves. Certain investments are impossible to postpone.[1]

Nevertheless, business firms which make allocations to investment reserves are naturally aware of the option that this gives them on future tax gains. In order to realize these gains they must be prepared to invest during periods when the reserves may be used. The system thus stimulates preparatory planning for investment expenditure and leads to a more rapid reaction when the reserves are released. An attractive aspect of the investment reserve system is that reliance is placed on a voluntary and cooperative relationship between government and business. Business firms are not required by law to set aside funds in investment reserves; they do so voluntarily with the knowledge that the government in granting certain tax inducements expects in return the use of reserve funds during a recession.

No economic stabilization measure is free from defects. Government public works programs, for example, have serious flaws. They are started slowly, are often chosen by political criteria instead of the marketplace mechanism, and cannot be stopped once a recession has been ended. The use of the tax credit and accelerated depreciation as countercyclical fiscal instruments also has many drawbacks.

The investment reserve is a useful addition to the kit of stabilizing

---

[1] In interviews with several managers of Swedish business firms, the author gained the impression that more lucrative investments were undertaken regardless of the time period, while more marginal investments were delayed in anticipation of an eventual release of the investment reserve funds. The investment reserve, however, was regarded as an important factor with respect to decisions to invest in certain projects during a recession. The author is of the opinion that a certain amount of investment, over and above that which would have occurred anyway, would have been undertaken.

devices. Since many factors contribute to recessions, a variety of stabilization techniques is more useful than a limited number.

It is doubtful that the investment reserve system can be used in the United States. The institutional differences between the United States and Sweden are too great to permit a transplanting of this device. There is much greater cooperation in Sweden between labor, management, and the government. There is the knowledge among the three groups that cooperation is necessary for survival in the world markets. Sweden is also much smaller than the United States both in terms of geography and population. Industrial concentration is largely limited to Stockholm and the southern part of Sweden. A much greater diversity in terms of industrial development and population growth exists in the United States. More industry and population is concentrated in New York than in all of Sweden. Nevertheless, devices similar to the investment reserve might be a helpful addition to the list of techniques which the United States has used to moderate the amplitude of industrial fluctuations.

APPENDIX

A. Depreciation Policy in Sweden

Sweden has also experimented with various depreciation methods. In 1938 a policy of free depreciation was adopted.[1] Under this policy, a corporation was allowed, for income tax purposes, to write off machinery and equipment as it saw fit. Thus, the entire cost, or any portion of it, which a corporation considered appropriate, could be written off as an expense in the year of acquisition of the asset, subject to two restrictions:

1. Depreciation for tax purposes in any year had to coincide with depreciation taken on the books for that year; and
2. In no case could total depreciation taken on the books and reported on the tax returns exceed the original cost of the asset.

However, in 1955 free depreciation was replaced by a more restrictive depreciation policy, for it was felt that the free depreciation system was contributing to inflation. The combination of high taxes and high profits induced some corporations to acquire capital items in order to increase depreciation allowances rather than for ordinary business reasons. This led to increased corporate spending and to more inflation at a time when the problem was to keep capital expenditures within the limits of available resources.[2]

---

[1] The 1938 provision had as its basic policy objective, the creation of a more nearly depression-resistant economy through the use of devices to stimulate investment.

·The free depreciation provision was limited to corporations, economic associations, savings banks, and mutual insurance companies. Individual proprietors and partnerships were restricted to the use of annual depreciation rates based on the estimated useful life of the item.

[2] The present Swedish system of investment reserves was introduced in 1955 as a partial compensation for the loss of free depreciation. The investment reserve scheme was introduced with the hope that it would be an effective instrument for stimulating business investment when needed, not otherwise.

The new system of depreciation, however, is quite flexible as an instrument of public policy. A brief summation of depreciation policy allowed in Sweden with respect to machinery and equipment is as follows:

1. The taxpayer may use a 30 percent declining-balance method which means that depreciation in any one year cannot exceed 30 percent of the year-end book value of the taxpayers' machinery and equipment. Under this rule, 30 percent of the cost of the equipment can be written off the first year, 30 percent of the remaining balance the second year, 30 percent of the remaining balance the third year, and by the end of the five years, the cost of the equipment has been written off. The 30 percent is the ceiling; the taxpayer can take less if he chooses—5 percent of book value one year, 30 percent the next year, and so on.

2. Instead of the 30 percent declining-balance method, a company may at any time take a straight-line deduction of 20 percent of the book value of its machinery and equipment. Under this rule, it can write off the cost of the machinery and equipment in five years.

In any particular year, the company can use either the declining-balance or straight-line method. However, whichever method is selected must be applied to all of the machinery and equipment. In other words, the declining-balance method cannot be applied to some items and the straight-line method to others. These methods and percentages apply only to machinery and equipment. Buildings are depreciated at straight-line rates which are often as low as 3 percent.

An example of the use of both the declining-balance and straight-line methods is as follows:

The cost of the machinery is assumed to be 100,000 kronor. The declining-balance method is used and 30 percent of the cost (30,000 kronor) is written off the first year. The balance is 70,000 kronor. For the second year, the declining-balance method is used, and 30 percent of the balance or 21,000 kronor is written off. The balance is reduced to 49,000 kronor. For the third year, 30 percent of this balance or 14,700 kronor is written off. The balance is now 34,300 kronor. For the fourth year, the straight-line method is used (20 percent of the original cost of the machinery) and 20,000 kronor is written off. The balance for the fifth year is now 14,300 kronor. The straight-line method is used and this is written off. As a percentage of the total cost of the machinery, the annual writeoffs are 30 percent, 21 percent, 14.7 percent, 20 percent, and 14.3 percent for the five-year period.

If the employment situation requires it, the Swedish government may decide that business firms which procure within a stipulated period of time machinery and equipment for permanent use in their own enterprises—agriculture, business, and forestry—by purchase or by producing it themselves, or sign a contract for future delivery, will be entitled to an extra depreciation allowance of 30 percent of the cost, in addition to the regular declining-balance or straight-line depreciation allowed under tax legislation. In addition, the taxpayers may deduct 10 percent of the cost from taxable profits in their income tax returns. When machinery is contracted for future delivery, the 10 percent deduction will be made for the fiscal year during which delivery has been made. The extra depreciation allowance and 10 percent deduction from taxable profits apply to both national and local income taxation.

The government has been given considerable discretionary powers. It may make the claim to tax benefits contingent on fulfillment of stipulated conditions, and it may extend the tax benefits to business firms throughout Sweden or in specified areas only. The government can also determine the kind of machinery and equipment procurement which can establish a claim to tax benefits. If the government wishes to promote the location of industry in specified areas, this tax incentive can be limited to taxpayers in these areas.

If the procurement of machinery has been financed by the withdrawal of money from an investment reserve fund, the tax benefits under the special depreciation allowance cannot be claimed.

For machinery and equipment delivered immediately upon placement of the order, the extra first-year allowance of 30 percent and the allowance available under the regular tax legislation· would amount to a total of 51 percent of the price in the fiscal year when the purchase was made. For example, assume the machinery cost 100,000 kronor. Using the regular declining-balance of 30 percent, the depreciation deduction would be 30,000 kronor. This would leave a balance of 70,000 kronor. The extra first-year allowance of 30 percent is applied to this balance. The deduction would be 21,000 kronor. The balance is now 49,000 kronor. Fifty-one percent of the cost of the machinery, or 51,000 kronor, has been written off.

B. The Advantages of Using Investment Reserves

The Swedish Ministry of Finance has compared the advantages to be gained from the use of an investment reserve relative to the use of ordinary depreciation allowances which can be used as an alternative. This comparison involves two companies. One company uses the investment reserve at its disposal to acquire an asset; the other company acquires a similar asset and writes it off using the most favorable combination of the declining-balance and straight-line methods of depreciation.

The benefits obtained by the company using the investment reserve include the initial gain, which is the difference between the 49 percent tax rate and the 46 percent of the reserve which has to be deposited in the Riksbank, the gain from the release of the reserve from the Riksbank, and the extra tax deduction amounting to 10 percent of the total reserve used.

The company without an investment reserve can make annual depreciation deductions in the future amounting to the cost of the asset. The discounted value of the future tax payments which this company escapes through the annual depreciations constitutes its major advantage.

Three types of assets are used to compare the results to be derived from using both methods:

1. Machinery which is to be depreciated as quickly as possible during a five-year period with the declining-balance method being used (30 percent of the balance) for the first years and the straight-line method (20 percent) being used for the remainder.

2. An industrial building that may be written off at 5 percent a year for 20 years which is the shortest depreciation period permitted in Sweden for this type of asset.

3. An industrial building that may be written off at 3 percent a year for a 33-year period, a normal depreciation period for this asset.

In the following example, the investment in a given asset is put at one million kronor. The benefits of the investment reserve to the company using it consist of repayment of money previously blocked in the Riksbank of 460,000 kronor (46 percent of one million) and a tax gain through the extra tax deduction which amounts to 49,000 kronor, based on the tax rate of 49 percent multiplied by 10 percent of one million kronor. However, the latter sum will not be received in cash until the company's tax assessment has been filed. Assuming an interest rate of 4 percent, this amount is discounted to a current value of 47,000 kronor (49,000 divided by 1.04).

The position of the company without an investment reserve is represented by the discounted value of the tax gain which arises from future depreciation allowances on the one million investment. This value varies inversely with the rate of interest and the length of the depreciation period.

	Machinery (5 years)	Building (20 years)	Building (33 years)
1. Position of company using the investment reserve:			
Access to Riksbank deposits	460,000 [1]	460,000 [1]	460,000 [1]
Discounted value of extra tax deduction	47,000	47,000	47,000
Total	507,000	507,000	507,000
2. Position of company using depreciation allowances: Present value of tax credit through future depreciation allowances	441,000 [2][3]	333,000 [2][4]	269,000 [2][5]
Net gain through the use of investment reserve	66,000	174,000	238,000

[1] At the time of the setting aside of the investment reserve, a tax relief was gained which amounted to 30,000 kronor (49 percent tax rate times 1 million, less the 46 percent deposited in the Riksbank or 490,000 minus 460,000). However, this tax gain has been realized before the release of the reserve.

[2] For machinery, a maximally favorable annual depreciation allowance of 30, 21, 14.7, 20, and 14.3 percent is used. This involves a combination of the declining-balance and straight-line methods. An after-tax rate of interest of 4 percent is used to discount the value of the tax credit through future depreciation allowances. For machinery, this amounts to 90 percent of the tax which is to be paid in the future. For buildings with a 20-year depreciation period (5 percent annual depreciation allowance), the corresponding percentage is 67.9, and for buildings with a depreciation period of 33 years, it is 54.9 percent.

[3] 490,000 times 0.90
[4] 490,000 times 0.679
[5] 490,000 times 0.549

The general effect of using an investment reserve is approximately equal to a tax credit of about 7 percent of the value of the investment expenditure in the case of machinery, about 17 percent in the case of buildings with a 20-year depreciation period, and about 24 percent in the case of buildings with a depreciation period of 33 years.

C. Accounting, Liquidity, and Profitability Aspects of Investment Reserves

Professor Sven-Erik Johansson of the Stockholm School of Economics has presented another way of describing the profitability of the investment reserve, vis-à-vis, normal depreciation allowances. His presentation is as follows:

> To use an investment reserve for its purpose simply implies that a depreciation of a maximum of 100 percent of the acquisition cost of a new investment, e.g., in buildings or machinery, is charged the investment reserve account during the year of acquisition. This depreciation is not deductible for tax purposes, but rather the company is permitted to withdraw the deposit (of 46 percent of the reserve utilized) in the Riksbank, and, furthermore, to make a special "investment deduction" in the tax return equal to 10 percent of the reserve utilized. The total liquidity effect is approximately the same as the one obtained by free depreciation. It should be observed, however, that the company may not make any normal deductible allowances for depreciation of an investment, which have been written off in the way described above. The tax savings from normal allowances for depreciation will thus be lost.

> The improvement of the profitability of an investment when written off by using the investment reserve method instead of being subject to normal tax depreciation is illustrated in the following example which is based on the following assumptions:

> (a) The investment reserve is used for a building with a cost of acquisition of _____ 100
> (b) Rate of normal tax depreciation (straight-line) _____ 2.5%
> (c) Tax rate _____ 50%
> (d) Cost of capital (after tax) _____ 8%
> (e) Net present value after tax is used as a profitability index.
> (f) Taxes are paid at the end of the year.
> (g) The cash returned by the Riksbank is received at the beginning of the year during which the investment is made.

Increases in the Net Present Value of an Investment in a
Building for Which the Investment Reserve is Used

	Present Value
Cash returned by the Riksbank (46 x 100)	46.0
Tax saving from the special "investment deduction" (.5 x .1 x 100 x .926)	4.6
Loss of tax savings from normal tax depreciation (.5 x .025 x 100 x 11.925)	(14.9)
	35.7

The net present value is thus increased by 35.7 percent of the
initial investment. Obviously, the higher the last item, the smaller
the increase in the present value. At a normal tax depreciation rate
of 20 percent (which is one of the standards used in Sweden for
machinery and equipment), the net advantage (in terms of present
value) of the disposition of the investment reserve is reduced to 10.7
percent of the initial investment.[3]

[3] Sven-Erik Johansson, "An Appraisal of the Swedish System of Investment Reserves," *International Journal of Accounting,* Fall, 1965, pp. 87-88.

BIBLIOGRAPHY

Official Swedish Publications

National Central Bureau of Statistics, *National Accounts, 1950-1965*, Statistical Reports, 1966.

Sekretariatet for Ekonomisk Planering, Konjunktur Läget, 1957, 1958, 1959, 1960, 1961, and 1962.

Sveriges Riksbank, Annual Reports for 1960, 1961, and 1962.

Books, pamphlets, and articles

Canarp, Curt. "Investment Funds—and How They Can Be Used to Combat Recession and Unemployment," *Skandinaviska Banken,* Quarterly Review, Vol. 44, No. 2, 1963.

Eliasson, Gunnar. *Investment Funds in Operation,* National Institute for Economic Research, 1965.

Johansson, Sven-Erik. "An Appraisal of the Swedish System of Investment Reserves," *International Journal of Accounting,* Vol. 1, No. 1, 1965.

Lundberg, Erik. *Business Cycles and Economic Policy* (Cambridge: Harvard University Press, 1957).

Mildner, Erwin, and Scott, Ira. "An Innovation in Fiscal Policy, The Swedish Investment Reserve System," *National Tax Journal,* Vol. 15, No. 3, 1962.

Narr, Martin. "Taxation and Stability: Guidance from Sweden," *Harvard Business Review,* January-February, 1960.

Nitare, Gideon. "Investment Reserves," National Labor Market Board, 1961.

Olsson, Bertil. "The Marginal Five Percent," *Columbia Journal of World Business,* Volume 1, 1965.

"Employment Policy During the Recession," *Skandinaviska Banken,* Quarterly Review, Vol. 40, No. 2, 1959.

Sandberg, Lars C. A Comment on "An Innovation in Fiscal Policy, The Swedish Investment Reserve System," *National Tax Journal,* Vol. 16, No. 1, 1963.

Schnitzer, Martin. "Unemployment Programs in Sweden," Joint Economic Committee of the U. S. Congress, Study Paper No. 5, 1964.

Shelton, John. "A Tax Incentive for Stabilizing Business Investment," *National Tax Journal,* Vol. 9, No. 3, 1956.

Vastnagan, Nils. "Tax Policy and Business Firms' Investment Activities," *Skandinaviska Banken,* Quarterly Review, Vol. 38, No. 3, 1957.

Wickman, Krister. "The Swedish Investment Reserve System, an Instrument of Countercyclical Policy," The Swedish Institute for Cultural Relations with Foreign Countries, 1964. Investeringarna och omsättningsskatten, Affärvärlden, 1963.

OTHER AEI PUBLICATIONS

BOOKS

CONGRESS AND THE PRESIDENCY: THEIR ROLE IN MODERN TIMES (First in series of 1966-67 Rational Debates). *Arthur M. Schlesinger, Jr.,* and *Alfred de Grazia,* 1967—$4.50

LAW, ORDER AND CIVIL DISOBEDIENCE (Second in series of 1966-67 Rational Debates). *Charles E. Whittaker* and *William Sloane Coffin, Jr.,* 1967—$4.50

INTERNATIONAL PAYMENTS PROBLEMS (Symposium proceedings)—1966 ($7.00)

Papers:

The International Payments System: Postwar Trends and Prospects, *Gottfried Haberler*

Internal Policies Compatible with External Equilibrium at Stable Exchange Rates, *Friedrich A. Lutz*

Exchange-Rate Flexibility, *James E. Meade*

The International Payments System: Is There a Shortage of International Liquidity? *Roy L. Reierson*

International Monetary Systems and the Free Market Economy, *Fritz Machlup*

CONGRESS: THE FIRST BRANCH OF GOVERNMENT—1966 ($6.50)

Monographs:

Toward a New Model of Congress, *Alfred de Grazia*

"Check and Balance" Today: What Does It Mean for Congress and Congressmen? *Lewis Anthony Dexter*

Congress and the Executive: The Race for Representation, *Roger H. Davidson*

The Service Function of the United States Congress, *Kenneth G. Olson*

Congressional Liaison, *Edward de Grazia*

Introducing Radical Incrementalism into the Budget, *Aaron Wildavsky*

The Committees in a Revitalized Congress, *Heinz Eulau*

Decision Making in Congress, *James A. Robinson*

Legislative Oversight, *Cornelius P. Cotter*

Availability of Information for Congressional Operations, *Charles R. Dechert*

Information Systems for Congress, *Kenneth Janda*

Strengthening the First Branch: An Inventory of Proposals

Congress: 1989, *Alfred de Grazia*

STUDIES

Japan: Prospects, Options, and Opportunities, *William J. Sebald* and *C. Nelson Spinks*—1967

Public Debt in a Democratic Society, *James M. Buchanan* and *Richard E. Wagner*—1967

Inflation: Its Causes and Cures, With a New Look at Inflation in 1966, *Gottfried Haberler*—1966

The U.S. Balance of Payments and International Monetary Reserves, *Howard S. Piquet*—1966 ($2.00)

The Federal Antitrust Laws, Revised Edition, *Jerrold G. Van Cise*—1965

The New United Nations—A Reappraisal of United States Policies, *George E. Taylor* and *Ben Cashman*—1965

French Planning, *Vera Lutz*—1965

The Free Society, *Clare E. Griffin*—1965, 138 pp. ($4.50)

Congress and the Federal Budget, *Murray L. Weidenbaum* and *John S. Saloma III*—1965, 209 pp. ($4.00)

Poverty: Definition and Perspective, *Rose D. Friedman*—1965

The Responsible Use of Power: A Critical Analysis of the Congressional Budget Process, *John S. Saloma III*—1964

Federal Budgeting—The Choice of Government Programs, *Murray L. Weidenbaum*—1964

The Rural Electrification Administration—An Evaluation, *John D. Garwood* and *W. C. Tuthill*—1963

The Economic Analysis of Labor Union Power, Revised Edition, *Edward H. Chamberlin*—1963

United States Aid to Yugoslavia and Poland—Analysis of a Controversy, *Milorad M. Drachkovitch*—1963

Communists in Coalition Governments, *Gerhart Niemeyer*—1963

Subsidized Food Consumption, *Don Paarlberg*—1963

Automation—The Impact of Technological Change, *Yale Brozen*—1963

Essay on Apportionment and Representative Government, *Alfred de Grazia*—1963 ($2.00)

American Foreign Aid Doctrines, *Edward C. Banfield*—1963

The Rescue of the Dollar, *Wilson E. Schmidt*—1963

The Role of Gold, *Arthur Kemp*—1963

Pricing Power and "Administrative" Inflation—Concepts, Facts and Policy Implications, *Henry W. Briefs*—1962

Depreciation Reform and Capital Replacement, *William T. Hogan*—1962

Consolidated Grants: A Means of Maintaining Fiscal Responsibility, *George C. S. Benson* and *Harold F. McClelland*—1961

*The Patchwork History of Foreign Aid, *Lorna Morley* and *Felix Morley*—1961

U.S. Immigration Policy and World Population Problems, *Virgil Salera*—1960

Voluntary Health Insurance in the United States, *Rita R. Campbell* and *W. Glenn Campbell*—1960

*United States Aid and Indian Economic Development, *P. T. Bauer*—1959

Improving National Transportation Policy, *John H. Frederick*—1959

The Question of Governmental Oil Import Restrictions, *William H. Peterson*—1959

Labor Unions and the Concept of Public Service, *Roscoe Pound*—1959

Labor Unions and Public Policy, *Edward H. Chamberlin, Philip D. Bradley, Gerard D. Reilly,* and *Roscoe Pound*—1958, 177 pp. ($2.00)

National Aid to Higher Education, *George C. S. Benson* and *John M. Payne*—1958

Post-War West German and United Kingdom Recovery, *David McCord Wright*—1957

The Regulation of Natural Gas, *James W. McKie*—1957

Legal Immunities of Labor Unions, *Roscoe Pound*—1957

*Involuntary Participation in Unionism, *Philip D. Bradley*—1956

*The Role of Government in Developing Peaceful Uses of Atomic Energy, *Arthur Kemp*—1956

*The Role of The Federal Government in Housing, *Paul F. Wendt*—1956

*The Upper Colorado Reclamation Project, Pro by *Sen. Arthur V. Watkins,* Con by *Raymond Moley*—1956

*Out of print.

LEGISLATIVE AND SPECIAL ANALYSES

89th Congress, Second Session, 1966

*Legislative History, 89th Congress, 1st Session, and Index of AEI Publications

Proposals for 4-Year Term for Members of the House of Representatives

*Proposals for Revision of The Electoral College System

The Federal Budget for the 1967 Fiscal Year

Proposed Amendment to the Fair Labor Standards Act. Bill by *Rep. Dent*

The New Veterans' Benefits Law

The "Freedom of Information" Bill. Bill by *Sen. Long (Mo.)*

Proposed Federal Unemployment Compensation Legislation of 1966. A supplement to AEI 1965 Analysis

Housing and Urban Development Bills. Bills by *Sen. Sparkman; Rep. Patman*

The Water Pollution Control Bill. Bill by *Sen. Muskie*

The "Truth in Packaging" Bill. Bills by *Sen. Hart; Rep. Staggers*

The Bill to Suspend the Investment Tax Credit for Machinery and Equipment. Bill by *Rep. Mills*

Foreign Aid Policy of the United States. National High School Debate Series. *Special Analysis*

Foreign Policy Commitments of the United States. National College Debate Series. *Special Analysis* ($2.00)

*Out of print.

90th Congress, First Session, 1967

Legislative History, 89th Congress, 2d Session, and Index of AEI Publications

The Federal Budget for the 1968 Fiscal Year

U.S. Foreign Trade Policy After the "Kennedy Round"

Proposed Social Security Amendments of 1967

A Convention to Amend the Constitution?—Questions Involved in Calling a Convention Upon Applications by State Legislatures. *Special Analysis*

Combating Crime. National High School Debate Series. *Special Analysis*

Unless otherwise indicated, all Studies and Analyses—$1.00 per copy.